THE
GENEROSITY
FACTOR™

THE
GENEROSITY
FACTOR™

DISCOVER *the* JOY *of* GIVING
YOUR TIME, TALENT, *and* TREASURE

KEN BLANCHARD
Coauthor of THE ONE MINUTE MANAGER®

— AND —

S. TRUETT CATHY
founder of CHICK-FIL-A®

ZONDERVAN.com/
AUTHORTRACKER
follow your favorite authors

ZONDERVAN

The Generosity Factor
Copyright © 2002 by Blanchard Family Partnership and STC Literary, LLC.

Requests for information should be addressed to:

Zondervan, *Grand Rapids, Michigan 49530*

This edition: ISBN 978-0-310-32499-7 (softcover)

Library of Congress Cataloging-in-Publication Data

Blanchard, Kenneth H.
    The generosity factor : discover the joy of giving your time, talent, and
treasure / Ken Blanchard and S. Truett Cathy.
       p.   cm.
    ISBN 978-0-310-24660-2 (hardcover)
    1. Corporations—Charitable contributions—Fiction. 2. Gifts—Moral and
ethical aspects—Fiction. 3. Generosity—Fiction. I. Cathy, S. Truett. II. Title.
    PS3552. L365134 G46 2002   200204151

Interior design: Beth Shagene

Printed in the United States of America

10 11 12 13 14 15 • 21 20 19 18 17 16 15 14 13 12 11 10 9 8 7 6 5 4 3 2

*To those with needs physical, financial, emotional,
and spiritual and to those who help meet them.*

Contents

THE CONTRADICTION

There's a saying of Jesus—reportedly more than two thousand years old—that goes like this: "It is more blessed to give than to receive."

But in our time, many in our society seem to be ruled by a contradictory principle: "Receiving is all that matters."

Other often-heard comments are:

- "Get all you can out of life."
- "Always look out for Number One."
- "We need more to fall to the bottom line."
- "I made mine. If you want yours, go earn it for yourself."
- "Only the strong survive."

Consider the way in which much of business is conducted in our day. Profits are plowed back into development in order to make the upcoming Initial Public Offering at the stock market more attractive. Rather than helping worthwhile causes, many who attain new wealth put their money into investment plans that they believe will increase their security in retirement. The gap between the rich and the poor seems to be widening. And charitable contributions have remained relatively level—at about two percent of our Gross Domestic Product despite the fact that we live in the era of the "new economy" in which more and more of us are prospering.

Is our world better for this?

Take a moment to answer these questions:

- Does every child in America and around the world go to bed with a full stomach and a loving hug from someone who cares?
- Is all of the possible research being done to cure devastating diseases?
- Can every qualified student afford a college education?
- Do the homeless have a warm place to rest their heads at night?

Some would argue that these problems don't belong to them. Their pat answers include:

- "I made it in life without anything being handed to me."
- "If they bothered to get a job, they wouldn't be homeless."
- "I worked my own way through college."
- "If we cure one disease, a new one will crop up anyway."
- "This is a job for the government."

But the truth is, a pat answer has never solved a problem. It takes dedicated people, devoted time, and donated dollars to solve problems.

Giving—of talent, time, and money—can hurt. It can mean sacrifice. An individual who gives may have to forego a new computer or season tickets to a favorite sporting event. A family that gives may have to pass on two extra days of their vacation or a bigger audio system in the new car. A corporation that gives may not be able to reassure its shareholders with the answers they demand. A church or synagogue that gives may have to forget about its own perceived needs for a new video projection system or some other elaborate, costly improvement to its facilities.

The flip side is that giving has tremendous rewards. These rewards can become evident in a variety of dimensions —emotional, relational, financial, and even spiritual.

It is our privilege to introduce you to the wondrous nature of those rewards. We invite you to join us on a journey to discover the joys of giving—and the impact that "the Generosity Factor™" can have on your life!

—KEN BLANCHARD AND S. TRUETT CATHY

I

THE BROKER

I LOVE HAVING MONEY, THE BROKER THOUGHT TO HIMSELF AS he stepped through the front door of his imposing Long Island home and into the brisk October morning. *And I love that I made it all on my own!*

The young, trim man with an athletic build was pleased that his limousine was parked as close to the entrance as possible. He pulled his coat collar up around his neck and rushed past the Driver, who held the car door open.

"Grab the three bags just inside the door, would you?" the Broker asked in a manner that suggested he fully anticipated that his request would be fulfilled without question. He seldom carried anything for himself these days; his computer bag, perhaps, but that was about it. He slid into the back seat and the Driver gently but securely closed the door.

A few seconds later, the Driver placed the bags in the trunk and got behind the wheel.

"Could you turn the heat up a bit?"

"Yes, sir," the Driver obliged.

The Broker picked up the copy of that day's edition of his preferred financial publication. It had been placed on the seat next to him—something he had come to expect in a matter-of-fact sort of way. He quickly flipped to page three to read his favorite biweekly column, "The Personal Side." This column was written by an engaging reporter who explored such topics as health and wellness, personal growth, diet, and exercise. The Broker could almost feel himself getting healthier as he read. "The Low-Carb Diet: Changing Your Metabolism" was the subject of the column.

The Broker had not always been this concerned about his personal health and well-being. As the heir to "old money"—though he had not yet inherited it—he was privileged to have been in the position to enjoy every advantage life had to offer. He attended a highly regarded graduate business school but may have attained his MBA more because of his father's financial support of the school than his own smarts.

That's not to say he didn't study hard throughout his college career. He studied hard between off-campus keggers. He studied hard between drug-laced parties and ski trips. He studied hard between binge weekends with fast young friends who did not have their futures in the forefront of their minds. He studied just hard enough to be awarded the parchment, although he ranked only in the dead middle of his class.

His father—hoping to leave a legacy in the financial world—invited the young, newly graduated Broker to join the family firm. *At worst*, the Broker thought at the time, *I'll have to work some. At best, I'll get a free ride.*

The Broker's father did his best to instill the old-fashioned work ethic in his son's life and career. As a result, there was no fast track. There was no instant partnership. There were no free-flowing raises and bonuses. There were no "spiffs" or special perks.

The Broker quickly verbalized his discontent. He attempted to talk to his father about it, but the "Old Man" would hear nothing of his son's pleadings.

Then, as if by magic, a stunning opportunity appeared on the young Broker's horizon—the Internet!

The Broker determined to start his own company—an online brokerage house that would handle trades over the faster and faster modems and DSL lines that were increasingly connecting America in instant fashion. And so, his firm was born and he left the comforts of his father's success.

The first year was a struggle. He lived in a cold apartment with walls of peeling paint in Brooklyn, a few blocks from the Verrazano Narrows Bridge. He took the train into Manhattan. He sat next to secretaries wearing sneakers, gang members wearing tattoos, and "suits" wearing suits.

His office was more than a few blocks off Wall Street, on the far east edge of the Village. It was nothing like his father's prestigious office with its panoramic view of the harbor that included a glimpse of the Statue of Liberty. No, the Broker's view was that of the fire escape hanging precariously from the dilapidated brick building that practically pressed against his window.

At first, his business saw little activity. Hits on his Web site were few and far between. *I may have made a huge mistake*, the Broker thought. *Maybe I should have hung in there with my father's firm, proven myself and worked my way up the ladder on his terms.*

But something happened to change it all. The Broker was watching a business report on television one day, and the founder of a competing "dot.com" online brokerage firm revealed the secrets of his success. They were so simple, so common sense and so easily implemented that the Broker jumped on the ideas immediately.

Within twenty-four hours of implementing the first stages of a cost-effective marketing plan, the traffic to the Broker's Web site increased exponentially. Within days he was running ads in *The New York Times* and *The Wall Street Journal* to recruit employees. Two weeks later, he concluded that running ads and screening prospects were counterproductive, so he contracted with an employment agency that specialized in the high-tech and high-finance fields.

His big move came next. A large space in a prestigious Wall Street office building opened up, the result of the merger of two firms. He snapped up the space and negotiated an option for additional footage.

Success was his. His without his father, his father's firm, and his father's old-fashioned ideas. "That Internet fad won't last a year," his father had warned him. Dad was wrong.

The Broker's thoughts and recollections of sweet victories were interrupted by the sound of the limousine's divider window being retracted.

"Will you want me to drop your bags at the apartment, or will you be needing anything from them?" the Driver asked.

"They can all go to the apartment," the Broker replied.

"Very well, sir. And will you be needing me for anything before Friday?"

"No ... oh, wait, I have dinner reservations Thursday night."

"And will we be picking up Miss Stephanie?"

"Of course. I'm going to be dining with Stephanie. Did you think I'd be escorting the bag lady who hangs out in front of my office building?"

"No, sir. I'm sorry, sir."

The Broker pressed a button and closed the divider. If there were two things that had floated to the top of his "could-do-without" list, it was that unkempt bag lady and prying chauffeurs. People in service positions were, in the Broker's opinion, on a need-to-know basis, with the need determined by the employer.

Still, the Driver had been with him almost from the moment his company took off, and was basically tolerable. Good drivers were, after all, in short supply—especially ones willing to work split schedules involving odd hours.

I pay him well enough, the Broker reassured himself as the limousine pulled up in front of his building, a stunning high-rise tower with views from his office that put his father's to shame.

Sure enough, the bag lady was there, surrounded by other street people who, as is their apparent custom, talked to her briefly and moved on.

I wish New York's Finest would do something about this situation, the Broker thought. "See you Thursday, 6:00 p.m., the apartment," the Broker said to the Driver. "We'll be having dinner at a French place on East 55th. L' Something-or-Other."

"Very well, sir."

The Driver stepped out into the rush of cars and hurried around the back of the vehicle to open the door for his employer.

Just before the Broker passed through the gleaming brass revolving door and into the marble-lined atrium of his office building, he looked up at the imposing structure that seemed to reach to heaven itself, and a disturbing thought crossed his mind:

I wonder why I feel so dreadfully insignificant.

2

THE DRIVER

IF THE BROKER WERE ABLE TO CHOOSE HIS PAST OR HIS PRESENT, he certainly would not have chosen the life that belonged to his driver.

The Driver, however, has never considered himself disadvantaged, although he could have justified such thoughts more easily than most. He was born to poor parents in one of the most impoverished areas of "America's Great Melting Pot."

His father was killed in a drug deal gone bad when the Driver was just twelve. It didn't matter much to him, though. His dad was an addict himself and used to beat the Driver's mother senseless without any provocation. Might have been a good thing he died and was gone forever.

The Driver survived his youth by becoming a fighter. He was meaner and tougher and more fearless than his peers. He had to be. His speech impediment had made him an easy target of ridicule. But the day he pummeled a police officer with repeated blows from his iron-like fists — sending the man to the hospital and ending his career on the force — the ridicule stopped.

He was sent to a detention center for that lapse in judgment, where he served six long, lonely years. During that time, a mentor stepped into his life. She was a teacher who volunteered evenings and weekends to tutor the young men in that institution. She taught them reading skills, basic math, the wonders of science, and even personal hygiene. But most of all, she built their self-esteem.

"Whh...whhy...why...d...d...do you even come hhh...here?" he demanded of her at first.

But as she touched his life with her listening ears, her tear-misted eyes, her soft words of encouragement, it suddenly occurred to him, *This must be what love is all about.*

Indeed, it was, though he had only seen glimpses of it from his mother. The Teacher was drawn to the young man. *He could amount to something*, she thought. She took extra time with him. She taught him about the kind of self-reliance that doesn't come at the expense of others. She convinced him that the day he was set free, he would never have to go back to his old ways.

She was right. Unlike so many ex-prisoners who quickly slip back into their former lives upon release, the Driver never returned to crime — or to punishment.

Today, the Driver is known as a gentle, caring man. He has a loving wife and five wonderful children. His oldest — his only daughter — is very bright and would be in college if finances permitted. Even with the scholarships that were available to her during her senior year in high school, the total package fell woefully short. These days she works hard cleaning the homes of those whose sons and daughters *are* in college.

The Driver is active in his neighborhood and his church. He serves on the crime watch committee and sings in the choir. He volunteers what little free time he has left to help former prisoners reconnect with life. It's his way of honoring the memory of the teacher who had come to his rescue. He'd do more, but he works the graveyard shift for an office maintenance company in order to keep his days and evenings free to drive for the Broker. There have been long stretches, though, where he's gotten barely enough sleep to get by. The Broker sometimes parties well into the night, forcing the Driver to be late for his maintenance job. On those occasions, the Driver's Daughter always seems able to come to the rescue at the last moment and handles the mop and bucket duties for her dad.

Everyone who knows the Driver thinks the world of him. They marvel at the fact that they've never heard a negative word slip past his lips. They wonder how a man with very little money — a man who struggles every day of his life — can manage a genuine smile and a warm word for every person he meets.

But this is no mystery to the Driver. He often wonders how anyone could live life any other way.

3

THE EXECUTIVE

LOOKS CAN BE DECEIVING. SO CAN FIRST IMPRESSIONS. To look at the Executive—to talk with him, walk with him—one would never guess that he is a wealthy man. One would never suspect that he had built a multi-state chain of auto parts and service centers from a simple idea in a single location. One would have no idea that his business provided jobs for thousands of people nor that the lobby of his headquarters building was home to an impressive collection of valuable, rare automobiles.

Despite his success, the Executive has never forgotten where he came from. He remembers what it's like to be poor. He remembers the struggles, the setbacks, the total failures.

He was born in the mid–1930s on a farm in Wisconsin to a family that had struggled through the depression years with barely enough money to survive. His father had become so discouraged that he simply gave up. One day he announced that he was going into town and he disappeared. Rumors suggested that he had taken his own life, but no evidence of that ever surfaced.

In an odd sort of way, the dad's departure was a blessing. He was never pleased with the efforts of his wife, three sons, or daughter. Every word the Executive heard was biting, bitter, and sarcastic. His dad seemed to enjoy catching his family doing things wrong and often resorted to a razor strap to express his displeasure with his children. The Executive-to-be found himself sleeping better at night after his dad was gone.

The Executive's mother continued to work the farm with the help of the Executive's two older brothers. Despite her hard life and long hours, his mom always made time to teach her children about life, to take them to church, and to encourage them to discover the difference faith could make in their lives.

The years passed. Life was relentlessly difficult for the family and money was always in short supply. When the soles of the kids' shoes were worn through, the mother stuffed cardboard inside to get more use out of them. Lunch at school consisted of whatever was left over from breakfast. She once sent the future Executive to the store—a two-mile walk into town—to buy some groceries "on account." He was sent home empty-handed and had to deliver the humiliating news to his mother that there would be no more groceries until past bills were settled.

When the Executive was old enough to comprehend the value of money, he decided to do something about his family's circumstances. He took odd jobs on his way home from school in order to contribute a few nickels here, a few quarters there. For several years, he sold *GRIT*, the venerable newspaper, door to door. He didn't make enough money to buy any luxuries, but he was able to help out with some of the necessities.

Despite hard work and long hours, the Executive still managed to stay in school until the tenth grade. He wanted to graduate, but the Korean Conflict erupted and his two older brothers were called to serve in the military. The Executive's strong back and quick mind were needed on the farm. He never had the opportunity to go back to high school or consider college. He simply worked.

After sunset, especially in the winter, there wasn't much that could be accomplished on the farm, so the Executive got a night job in town—pumping gas, changing oil, and doing grease jobs at a service station. There he learned a number of valuable skills—not just mechanical skills, but "people skills" as well. He discovered the importance of customer service. His customers noticed his winning smile, attention to detail, and sparkling clean windshields—so much, in fact, that word circulated throughout the area and new customers would drive a few extra blocks past the competition in order to have "that fine young man" service their cars.

One April night as the Executive was changing into his uniform to head for work, there was a knock at the door. When he walked into the living room, he saw two men in military dress bearing somber expressions on their faces. His mother had collapsed on the sofa and was sobbing uncontrollably. One of the soldiers approached the Executive and delivered the bad news in hushed tones: "I'm sorry to inform you that your brother was wounded in action in Korea. He was evacuated to a military hospital for medical attention, but he died en route. There was nothing anyone could do. His remains will be shipped back to you as soon as possible."

"As soon as possible" took what seemed like an eternity. Unfortunately, the Executive's other brother wasn't able to get back from Korea for the funeral. Throughout the ordeal—the waiting, the viewing, the church services, the burial, and the inevitable period of mourning—the

Executive's mother was amazingly strong and imparted her strength to her son and daughter. "God has a plan," she said. "We just have to learn how to trust Him, even though we don't always understand."

Despite her words of comfort, the Executive missed his brother immeasurably. He could have become bitter, just as the Driver could have become had he chosen that destructive path. But instead, he decided to honor his brother's memory the only way that he knew how. At the age of nineteen, he proudly enlisted in the U.S. Army. Love of country meant a lot to him then. It still does today.

By the time he left for boot camp, the fighting in Korea had ended and most of the troops had returned, including his surviving brother, who quickly assumed all of the responsibilities on the farm.

The Executive was eventually stationed at Fort Carson, just south of Colorado Springs, Colorado, and was assigned to the motor pool. He seemed to be a natural at mechanics and could tear down any engine or transmission, diagnose the problem, and rebuild the unit so that it performed better than new.

Within weeks of his arrival at his base, he had fallen in love—twice. He fell in love with the breathtaking beauty of Colorado, and he was completely swept away by the loveliness of a young Army nurse named Carolyn. It only took one look—and three dates—for the Executive to propose. They were married in a small ceremony during a short leave and moved into newly constructed family housing at Fort Carson.

Carolyn was discharged from the Army several months before the Executive, so they decided it was a good time to start a family. Their first son was born in good health, and both mom and dad were excited and happy.

The Executive, of course, kept in touch with his mother, brother, and sister by phone and mail, and had promised to return home after his discharge to help run the farm. His brother, though, had since gotten married and had enrolled in night school under the GI Bill. His objective was to become a teacher. With a mixture of regret and relief, his mother decided to sell the farm to free her son to pursue his dream. She moved to a small house in town—a decision that her three children agreed was a wise one.

Once out of the Army, the Executive and his wife moved to Denver, where he got a job as a mechanic at a large service station. He was quickly promoted to assistant manager. Less than a year later, the owner decided to retire and structured a financing plan that allowed his most valued employee to purchase the station.

The Executive was now on his way to becoming an "executive." In fact, under his ownership, the operation became wildly successful. The Executive soon purchased another station, added to the building, and began to offer parts and tires in addition to mechanical repairs. Realizing that he was onto something, the Executive began to train his best employees to manage the operation. That way, he could continue to build new service centers in Denver and across Colorado.

The eventual outcome? He now has more than eight hundred auto service centers and parts outlets scattered throughout the southwestern United States.

But there is something different about the Executive. Instead of hoarding his money, instead of being driven by the desire for wealth, he took a different approach. It was so foreign to conventional thinking that he began to attract some attention.

One October Thursday, an invited visitor stopped by the Executive's office. She was armed with a small tape recorder, a pen, and a notepad. She set the tape recorder on the Executive's desk and pressed "record." She asked questions. She made notes. And she quickly realized that she had hit on something big.

4

THE COLUMN

THE BROKER HAD ENJOYED A PICTURE-PERFECT WEEKEND. HE took his boat out to the deep seas on an unusually balmy and beautiful October day and caught a fish that was destined to be a trophy. He hosted a party that was sure to make the social news in the more "gabby" of the New York newspapers. Several of New York's leading executives were on his guest list, and to his great satisfaction, they all showed up. *They must know a true market maker when they spot one*, he reasoned.

The Broker rolled out of bed Monday morning after hitting the sleep button only three times. Must not have been as grand a party as he originally thought.

He lifted weights, took a quick shower, shoveled down a large bowl of bran flakes, and headed for the door. New conquests lay ahead, he was certain.

Sure enough, his limousine was there in the driveway waiting for him. So was his favorite financial newspaper. He picked it up and immediately turned to page three. His favorite column jumped out at him. So did a whole new way of looking at life.

The Broker had expected to read another article about health and fitness. "The Benefits of Therapeutic Massage" might have been an appropriate subject following his weekend of deep-sea fishing and other muscle-stressing activities.

Instead, he discovered that the Reporter's column was about a gentleman from Denver—a man who must be in his sixties or seventies, judging from the picture—who claimed that the greatest joy in his life was his ability to give to others.

What kind of nonsense is this? the Broker thought to himself as he boarded the elevator and rose high above the teeming city with its traffic jams and bag ladies and homeless people and struggling hot dog vendors.

Still, the article stuck with him through the entire morning. Finally, after a hurried lunch of carryout Thai food that he consumed at his desk, he couldn't stand it any longer. He called his favorite financial publication and asked to speak to his favorite Reporter. To his surprise, she was in her office and took his call without hesitation.

"How's the Internet brokerage business?" the Reporter asked upon picking up her phone.

"Amazing," the Broker responded in shock. "How do you know who I am?"

"I try to keep up on what's hot and happening."

"I'm impressed!"

"What's on your mind?" the very direct Reporter asked.

"You're perceptive. There *is* something on my mind."

"Perceptiveness is half my job."

The Broker laughed. "Well, you're certainly good at that half!" Then he shifted to a serious tone. "This Executive you wrote about in today's column—is he for real?"

"Sure is. I flew to Denver and met with him personally. He really believes that generosity is the answer to the question, 'What Is the Meaning of Life?'"

"I don't buy it," the Broker responded emphatically.

"Hey, I'm not trying to make a convert out of you. I'm just a reporter. But if you met him, you probably *would* 'buy it,' as you put it."

"I guess I'll have to take your word for it. I'll never have the opportunity to meet the man."

"If it's important for you to find out for yourself, I imagine he'd be happy to meet with you."

"You're kidding!"

"Not at all. When I first heard about him, I dialed the number at his office and was put right through."

The Broker hesitated. A number of thoughts ran through his mind. One of them was, *Why would a success-ful executive take calls from strangers without having them screened first?*

The Reporter broke the awkward silence. "You want his phone number or not?"

"Well, if you have it handy."

She did. The Broker entered the number in his palm-top computer, expressed his thanks to the Reporter, and put the phone handset back in the cradle. His first impulse was to pick up the phone immediately and call the Execu-tive. But he thought better of that idea.

About mid-afternoon, the Broker's curiosity overpow-ered him. He grabbed the phone and dialed the Executive's number.

"I'll put you right through," the receptionist respond-ed cheerfully.

She's got to be kidding, the Broker thought to himself. *I'll be talking to his administrative assistant, I'm sure.*

The Broker waited. And waited some more. *I'll be lucky to talk to anyone, let alone his assistant. Probably lunch time in Denver, anyway.*

"I'm sorry," were the next words the Broker heard. It was the Executive himself. "I was on the other line. It was one of my grandkids. He wanted to tell me about something that happened in school today. I have more than a hundred grandchildren, you know."

A hundred grandchildren? Who has a family that big these days? Well, I guess if he can talk to his grandkids about trivial school matters, he can talk to me, the Broker decided.

"Thank you for taking my call," the Broker said.

"What's on your mind, friend?" the Executive asked.

"I read the article about you...."

"Yes, I know. The Reporter called to tell me I could expect to hear from you. I said I was looking forward to talking to you. I've read about you, you see."

"Really?"

"Yes, you're quite the success, from what I can tell."

"Thank you. I work hard at it, just as you have done for so many years. What I want to know is if you really said all those things ... if you really believe all those things ... about giving."

"Absolutely!"

"Why do you do it? Why do you give so much of your hard-earned money away? Wouldn't you rather leave it to your heirs or something?"

"Oh, I've provided for my heirs. But I have thousands of other special friends who need my help."

"Special friends? Thousands?" The Broker didn't understand what he had heard. "Can you explain?"

"Afraid I can't."

"Can't, or won't?" the Broker asked boldly.

"I can't explain all of this in words. I don't think you'd really understand. In your head maybe, but not in your heart. I'd have to show you." The Executive paused to rethink his answer. "Truth is, I couldn't even show you. You'd have to follow me around for a day and see for yourself. That's the only way you'd ever understand."

Even the Broker was surprised at the words that escaped his lips. "I want to do that!"

"Do you ever get to the Denver area?" the Executive inquired.

"As a matter of fact, I'm going to be there for a conference on high-tech investing in a couple of weeks. Let me check the exact dates."

The Broker touched the calendar button on his palmtop computer and it sprang to life. He scrolled through the dates and found his notes on the conference. "I'll be in Denver two weeks from tonight—and I'm staying Tuesday, Wednesday, and Thursday."

"Let me check my calendar real quick," the Executive offered. The Executive flipped through the pages of his old-fashioned, low-tech planner book. "If you could extend your trip through Friday, I could spend much of the day with you. It'll be a very full day, but I think it would explain a lot."

The Broker checked his palmtop again. He had a date with Stephanie that Saturday night—he had managed to come up with a pair of hard-to-get tickets for the hottest new show on Broadway—but there was nothing on his schedule for Friday that couldn't be moved to another day.

"You're on," he announced to the Executive.

"You'll have to be at my office early. I have a lot of special people to see."

"I'll be there."

The Broker hung up his phone and stared at it, dumbfounded. *I must be an idiot. What have I just done?*

He called his assistant into his office. "Could you do me a favor and change my return flight from the Denver conference to Friday? Make it a late flight. Oh, and add Thursday night to my hotel reservation and make sure the limousine is booked for an additional day."

"I'm on it," his assistant said. "Mind if I ask why you're staying an additional day?"

"Not at all. I'm simply going to prove for myself that someone doesn't really exist. There's no way he could, in fact."

The days didn't pass quickly enough to suit the Broker. He was not only looking forward to the investment conference, but he was also eagerly anticipating his meeting with the Executive.

The Broker's assistant rang him on the intercom.

"Your car is here."

He stuffed his laptop computer into a sleek Zero Halliburton case, extended the handle on his large suitcase, and headed toward the elevator. On his way out the front door, he nearly tripped on the bag lady. *I've had enough of this*, he thought angrily.

To his considerable surprise, it was not his Driver who held the door open for him.

"Who on earth are you?" he blurted out. "Where's my Driver?"

"I'm his Daughter," replied a young woman who appeared to be barely out of her teens.

"Where is he?"

"I'm sorry, sir. Please get inside the car, sir. It's kinda brisk out here, sir."

The Broker settled into the back seat as the young woman closed the door and put the larger of the bags in the trunk. When she had gotten behind the wheel and shifted the car into gear, he rolled the divider down.

"I asked, where is your father?" he restated with considerable firmness.

"He's with my mother," was her timid reply. "She's very sick. She's going to need surgery. I wanted to be with her, too, but my Daddy said I needed to drive you 'cuz he couldn't."

"Sorry to hear that. You know how to get to JFK?"

"I do, sir."

The Broker paused for a moment. This wasn't a part of his plan for the day, but he resolved to make the best of it.

"So, you going to school?" the Broker asked, in an attempt to make polite conversation.

"Nope, I work. My family ... well, we're lucky to graduate high school."

"Where do you work?"

"Lots of places. I clean houses. I guess you could say I'm a servant. Not that there's anything wrong with being a servant."

"No, I suppose not."

"They say I do a good job. That makes me happy."

The Broker was distracted by traffic. "Take the Midtown Tunnel," he suggested. "Fastest route this time of day, I've found."

"Yes, sir."

The Broker had participated in as much small talk as he wanted, and decided to sift through some papers in his brief case.

"I have some work to do."

"Fine, sir."

The Broker rolled the divider up. Then he had second thoughts and rolled it back down for a moment.

"Thanks for taking over for your father," he said.

"No problem. In our family we all help each other out. It's the way we do things."

"Well, thanks anyway," the Broker said as he reestablished his privacy behind the divider.

As the car crawled through the noisy rush hour traffic, the Broker's thoughts flashed back to the bag lady. *I've had enough of her.* He picked up his cell phone and dialed the number for directory assistance.

"NYPD, please ... No, I don't know which precinct ... south Manhattan ... Wall Street ... thank you."

The Broker waited for the automatically assisted connection to take place. A desk sergeant answered.

"I'm calling to report a public nuisance," the Broker began, firmness and distaste evident in his voice. "There's a vagrant who persists in hanging out in front of my office building. She's constantly harassing my employees and ruining my business. I want her arrested. Yes, I'd be willing to sign a complaint. Fax it to me and I'll fax it right back. Here's the fax number in my car."

And with that, the hardest, coldest man in New York went off to meet someone who may well be the most tenderhearted man in Denver.

5

ANTICIPATION

THE BROKER USUALLY CONSUMED TWO OR THREE COCKTAILS on flights of this duration—and four or more on any flight that navigated over a large body of water. But on this trip to Denver, he passed on the customary two or three. Instead, he made notes on his palmtop. He wanted to make sure he asked the right questions. He hoped the Executive would give him at least an hour or two of his time, but if not, he wanted to make sure his questions were clearly organized and extremely pointed.

The flight arrived on time—by airline standards, any-way—and, sure enough, the Broker was greeted at the gate by a uniformed chauffeur, just as he had requested. During the long drive from the airport to the hotel, the Broker learned more about the chauffeur than he had anticipated. Seems the young man was the Bible-thumping type who aspired to an acting career. It's not that the young man was abrasive or offensive. His demeanor could better be described as enthusiastic. The Broker found himself liking the young man despite himself.

"Do you need help getting your bags to your room?" the young chauffeur asked.

"No thanks. I'll have the bellman handle it."

"Will you be needing my services later?"

"No, my conference is right in the hotel. I don't think I'll need you until Friday morning. I need to be at the Executive's office by 8:00 or so."

"Friday at 8:00? I'll be here by 7:30 sharp, then."

The Broker was too worked up to sleep, so he unlocked the mini-bar in his room and had one of the cocktails that he had denied himself on the flight. He phoned the front desk to arrange for a wakeup call, watched *Headline News*, and eventually drifted off.

The conference turned out to be one of the best he had ever attended. The presenters really understood high tech, and offered forecasts of the future that stretched his imagination well beyond anything he could have anticipated.

When Friday morning arrived, the Broker was pleased to discover that the young chauffeur was waiting for him outside the front door of the hotel. Less than a half-hour later, the car was moving along the winding roads through the Executive's expansive corporate headquarters property.

"Sure is beautiful land," the young chauffeur volunteered.

"Sure is. Does he own all this?"

"I expect so. I hear that he didn't want every inch of land of suburban Denver to be bulldozed and built up with houses, high-rise apartments, and condos. So he bought much more than he needed, built his office building, and preserved the rest for trees and ponds and trails."

"He did a good job of it," the Broker affirmed. "Great views of the mountains."

As promised, the Broker arrived at the Executive's office building at 8:00 A.M. And, indeed, that's when the workday began. It's also when the Reporter's article began to come to life, right before the Broker's eyes.

6

THE OPEN DOOR

THE BROKER COULDN'T TAKE HIS EYES OFF THE ANTIQUE AND collector automobiles that filled the first floor lobby of the Executive's office building.

"Absolutely magnificent," he commented to the Executive's Assistant as he paused to admire a Lamborghini Countach that looked as though it had been driven directly from the showroom to this exact spot.

"It is, isn't it?" the Executive's Assistant agreed.

The Broker surveyed the other vehicles in the extensive collection. "He must really worship cars."

"Oh, no, not at all."

"Huh?"

"I'm serious. Despite the fact that our business is all about serving people who own automobiles, I think he displays all of these extraordinary machines here simply to inspire us."

"Okay," the Broker admitted. "You've lost me there."

"Think about it," the Executive's Assistant suggested. "Each of these cars is unique. The Executive regards each of his coworkers as unique. Each of these cars is prized—in the same way every one of us is prized by him. Every car is of equal value to him, no matter the age, the condition, or the miles on the odometer. He values each of us in the same way."

"He must be a very special person," the Broker speculated.

"Oh, he is. He most certainly is!"

They boarded the elevator and rode to the top floor. As they walked down the long passageway that overlooked the atrium, the Broker couldn't help but comment on the fact that nearly all of the office doors were wide open.

"We believe in a highly collaborative work environment," the Executive's Assistant said. "That could never happen if we conducted our business behind closed doors. Everyone here knows what's going on in other departments. We all have access to the kinds of information that many companies try to keep from their employees. That helps us understand that our individual contributions do have a significant impact."

All the Broker could say was, "Remarkable."

They arrived at the door to the Executive's office. It, too, was wide open. The Executive's Assistant motioned to the Broker to enter.

"Shouldn't we announce ourselves?" the Broker asked.

"Oh, he knew you'd show up first thing this morning. He's looking forward to meeting you."

"Why?"

"It's simple, really. He wants to let you in on his secret, so you can change your world as he's changed his."

7

THE SEEDS OF SIGNIFICANCE

THE EXECUTIVE EXTENDED HIS BIG HAND WARMLY. "GOOD to meet you," he said with a broad grin as he shook the Broker's hand. "Please feel free to take off your jacket and get comfortable. We don't go much for business suits around here. Too much cowboy in us, I guess."

"Thanks," the Broker said as he shed his jacket, loosened his tie, and settled into a big overstuffed chair.

"I understand you've come to learn about giving—about the impact that generosity has had on my own life," the Executive began.

"That's right," the Broker responded. "The article I read said that you believe that giving is one of the most important things you do."

"True. I believe giving is so important that I've developed a plan that actually makes it a tremendous pleasure to give. I call it 'the Generosity Factor,' and I use every opportunity I can to share the plan with others."

"Tremendous pleasure in giving?" the Broker wondered aloud. "That certainly doesn't fit with the way most people give. Usually giving is done out of guilt. Or a sense of obligation. Or to be the subject of a write-up in the newspaper."

"You forgot one," the Executive added. "Some give to reduce taxable income."

The Broker chuckled. "That's the big one for most of the people I know."

"We've been talking about money here, but there are actually four things you can give, and, in my mind, they are all of equal significance."

The Executive paused, walked over to the window overlooking a beautiful stand of trees on his expansive property, and gazed toward the mountains as if he were reflecting on all of the moments, large and small, that were woven together into the tapestry of his life. The Broker began to get a bit impatient. He wanted to keep the conversation moving. After all, he had a life waiting for him back in New York. He fiddled with his palmtop computer and scrolled through his list of prepared questions.

"Here they are," the Executive finally said as he turned away from the window. He spoke slowly and deliberately, as if he were expecting the Broker to take notes on his little electronic device. "Time. Talent. Treasure. Touch. Nothing more than these four. The beauty of it is, there are so many ways to give them. The tragedy is that so few people discover ways to give even one—let alone four."

The Broker thought about this for a moment. "I can understand how someone in your position could give treasure, but I can't understand giving anything beyond that. You and I are overextended business people with responsibilities to our employees and customers. I know that in my position, I could never give time or talent. How is it that you can?"

It seemed as though the Executive had somehow anticipated the question and was ready with his answer. "I've lived many years and enjoyed so many blessings. And I believe that because much has been given to me, I owe much in return. I also believe that we can all find time to do the things we enjoy. I enjoy discovering ways to meet the needs of others, so I make time for that."

Is this all talk, or does he actually invest his time? the Broker wondered.

The Executive interrupted his thoughts. "You're wondering if I actually do that."

"Well, yes. How did you know?"

"A lot of folks say they care about people, but they don't actually do anything about it. Generosity is all about caring about the needs of others, then acting to meet those needs. Time meets a certain kind of need. Talent meets another. Treasure still another, and touch meets its own set of needs. Generosity is about balance—about making all of one's resources available."

"You're going to have to explain that further."

"As I told you on the phone, I can't really explain it at all. I have to show you. That's the only way to convince you how important generosity really is. It's vital to those to whom you give, of course. But it's a life-changer for you."

"So what do we do next?" the Broker wondered.

"I want to take you for a drive," the Executive offered. "I want to introduce you to some of the best people on earth."

8

THE RIGHTS OF OWNERSHIP

THE BROKER SAT QUIETLY AS THE EXECUTIVE NEGOTIATED HIS beautifully restored '65 Pontiac GTO onto a busy Denver freeway. *This car is older than I am*, the Broker thought.

A few miles later, the Executive took an off-ramp, made a couple of quick right turns and pulled into the parking lot of an auto parts store and service center. As they walked through the door, the Broker glanced at a sign that displayed the hours of operation. The words "Closed Sundays" appeared near the bottom of the sign. *Odd*, the Broker thought. *How can they remain competitive if they're closed one day a week?*

The Executive led his guest to the service counter and asked if the Manager was in.

"He's in, sir, but I think he's out on the floor," replied the friendly young woman behind the counter. "May I tell him your name?"

The Executive told her, and the young woman was totally embarrassed. "I'm SO sorry I didn't recognize you, sir. I'll get my Manager right away!"

"Thank you," the Executive said with a smile. "And don't worry about not recognizing me. Happens all the time."

As the young woman left and the Executive led his guest to the comfortable customer waiting area, the Broker commented, "I read in the article that you own over eight hundred of these centers."

"There are 824, but I don't actually own them. It's more accurate to say that they've been entrusted to me."

"You must be really proud of your accomplishments," the Broker suggested. "You started with one gas station and now you own all these service centers, all those beautiful cars, your magnificent office building ... you own it all."

"As I started to explain, I don't own any of it," the Executive responded.

"You're kidding, right?"

"No, sir. I don't own anything. Not a bit of it."

"Who does, then? Your stockholders? Investors? Venture capitalists?"

"No, sir."

"Your employees, then? Do you have an Employee Stock Ownership Plan in place?"

"No again. He owns it all," the Executive answered softly.

"He? Who is he?"

"Why, God, of course."

"Sir, excuse me, but God doesn't figure in the world of business. The world of religion maybe, but not business."

"He figures in my world. That's why I close all my stores on Sundays. Gives our team members time for their families. Time to worship, if they choose to."

"This all seems kind of ... Bible-beltish."

The Executive smiled. "You're not interested in the spiritual aspects of life?"

The Broker thought before he spoke, then offered his best explanation. "It's been my experience that people who have achieved great things are successful because of hard work, highly refined skills, and a bit of old fashioned luck. In my case, I am the product of all three. I was born to money—my good fortune—but I also work hard and I'm very cunning."

"So you're a success without God?"

"Right," the Broker replied with confidence.

"Do you know anything about Him?"

"To be honest, I've only been in a church three or four, maybe five times in my life. My grandmother's funeral. My sister's wedding. A friend's wedding. The Bar Mitzvah of my best friend in junior high school. I guess that was at a synagogue, not a church per se."

"Fortunately, knowing God doesn't have all that much to do with going to churches, cathedrals, synagogues, or mosques. Knowing God takes place in the heart. I discovered a long time ago that if my heart was filled with greed and ambition, there was no room left for God. So I gave Him my heart, my possessions, my talents, and my time. Then He told me, 'Since you've given it all to me, I know I can trust you to manage it.'"

The Broker was beginning to wonder why he was wasting his time with this man in Denver. "God talks to you?" he asked in a condescending manner.

The Executive had a ready reply. "He doesn't wake me up with a shout in the middle of the night and tell me what to do the next day."

"Good. I didn't think so," the Broker interrupted.

"... but," the Executive continued, "He does tell me through His Word."

"His word?"

"The Bible."

The Broker was incredulous. "The Bible? Oh, come on! I'm sure the Bible is a wonderful collection of interesting myths and legends, but that's about it."

"I know a lot of people who think the way you do. But every single person I know who believes and trusts in the teachings of that old book has never been disappointed."

"Okay, I'll admit I don't really know what it teaches. I didn't pick up much at funerals, weddings, and Bar Mitzvahs."

"I believe you'd be amazed by the wisdom you'd find in it. In my case, the Bible serves as my inspiration, my guide, my compass, and it even provides the foundation on which I've built my business. I believe that biblical principles make great business principles."

"That's a tall order for an old book—one that was written centuries before radio, television, computers, the Internet...."

"It *is* a tall order, but it has lived up to all of my expectations. It has taught me that every good and perfect gift comes from God. In one place it says, 'Wealth and honor come from You; You are the ruler of all things.' It has taught me, too, that it is more blessed to give than to receive."

The Broker was perplexed. "So what does this all mean?"

"For me, it's very simple," the Executive explained. "If I have time on this earth, it's a gift. If I have any talents, they are gifts, too. Any money I have is a gift. And I don't believe that gifts are only to be received. They are meant to be given to others. To be shared. But the beautiful thing about all of this is that the rewards I receive outweigh anything I could ever give."

"Rewards? What do you mean? Articles in newspapers? Praise from others? Your name on a list of donors in a theater program? Bigger profits?"

"No, no, it's nothing like that. My rewards come in the form of smiles from children. Young people who are able to pursue their dreams. Kids who can go to camp. Team members who have a sense of fulfillment."

"I'd have to see this to believe it," said the skeptical Broker.

The Executive glanced out of the corner of his eye and noticed the Manager approaching them.

"I'd be happy to oblige! You can witness it right now."

"So good to see you!" the Manager exclaimed. "It's always a treat to have you stop by."

The Executive introduced the Broker and the Manager.

"It's a pleasure to meet you," the Manager offered.

"Same here," the Broker responded.

The Manager turned his attention to the Executive. "What brings you here today?" he asked.

"I have envelopes I'd like to personally present to a couple of your team members." The Executive took out two white envelopes and handed them to the Manager. "Either of these people in today?"

The Manager looked briefly at the names on the envelopes and gave them back to the Executive. "As a matter of fact, they both are. But I've never seen you personally hand these out before."

"You might say this is a special occasion. I'm teaching the Broker about the generosity factor, and I thought I could demonstrate with a personal visit."

The Manager led the Executive and the Broker back into the parts area as the Broker whispered, "What's going on?"

"You'll see," the Executive whispered back.

The Manager brought two young team members to the Executive and introduced them. They were both wearing wide grins—this was the first time they had met the Executive.

"Pleased to meet you," the Executive began. "Your Manager tells me that you both work hard and you do everything possible to take care of your customers. We all appreciate that. Service is what we're all about."

"Thank you," they gushed.

"Your Manager also tells me that you're both enrolled in college. As I'm sure you know, when you've served our company and our customers for as long as both of you have, we like to help you with your college expenses." The Executive handed an envelope to each of the team members. Inside each envelope was a check for $1,000, made payable to the colleges they were attending. They grinned and proudly held up their checks for the other team members to see. There was a spontaneous round of applause.

The Broker took the Manager aside and spoke softly. "Does he do this kind of thing often? Give out checks for a thousand dollars?"

"He doesn't usually hand the checks to them personally, but, the fact is, the company has given out over 16,000 of these scholarships."

"Sixteen *thousand?*" the Broker was dumbfounded. "Why, that's ... that's ..."

The Manager finished the math problem. "Sixteen million dollars."

9

FINDING OPPORTUNITIES

THE EXECUTIVE MERGED HIS CAR WITH THE FREEWAY TRAFFIC as the Broker sat in silence, contemplating what he had just witnessed at the service center. Finally, he blurted out the question that was uppermost in his mind. "Why do you do it? Why do you give college scholarship money to people you've never met?"

So much to teach this young man, the Executive thought as an impish grin crossed his face. "A generous person quickly discovers that each new day provides new opportunities to impact the lives of others. Every day we can find countless ways—great and small—to make someone's life better."

The Broker protested. "You've already given your employees jobs—why give them more?"

"Generosity isn't about doing the minimum—simply doing the expected. Every day I look for opportunities to do something extra. I make it a part of my routine. Kind of a habit, you might say."

"I'm afraid I don't understand," the Broker admitted.

"Some people think of generosity as an event. They get behind some cause and participate in an annual fund drive.

When their big splash is over, it's back to business as usual. But generosity is an attitude. It has to be cultivated daily."

"I see," the Broker said, knowing deep down that he didn't really see. "I really appreciate your time. You've taught me a lot about generosity in the past couple of hours."

"Oh, we're not done yet. Far from it. If you really want me to show you what the generosity factor is all about, you'll have to spend a couple of days with me."

"You want me to stay until tomorrow?"

"If you want to head back to New York now, you'll never discover the keys to the generosity factor," the Executive said, challenging the young man.

"I do want to know the secret," the Broker admitted. "Where to next?"

"We're going to visit my children."

The Broker pondered the meaning of this as the Executive left the freeway and drove through a comfortable but quite ordinary neighborhood. He pulled up in front of a large ranch-style house, honked the horn a few times, and stepped out of the car. In an instant, three young children — two boys and a girl, all of whom appeared to be under five years old — dashed out into the chilly mountain air, ran toward the Executive, and smothered him with hugs and kisses. "Grandpa! Grandpa!" they screamed with joy.

The Executive sat down on the front steps, hugged them individually, and told them how much he loved them.

"Did you bring us a present?" they asked excitedly.

"Yes, I did. I brought you an invisible present. It's here in my heart, and it's called love." He winked at the Broker, then fished in his pockets for three small candies. "I also brought you some treats."

"Thanks, Grandpa," they all said as they devoured the candy.

"I have something else for you," he said as he dug through his other pocket. He pulled out three shiny quarters. "I have some more quarters for your collections. You don't have your Georgia quarters yet, do you?"

"No, " they replied.

The Executive pointed to the nearly microscopic words that surrounded the state map of Georgia on the back side of the coin. "See these words here? They say 'Wisdom, Justice, and Moderation.' These words mean that we have to be smart and do our best, we have to be fair, and we have to live life in balance."

"What's balance, Grandpa?"

"Well, that's kind of hard to explain. But I think it means that if we get something from someone, we should give something in return. And that we don't do too much of one thing and not enough of another."

"I still don't understand."

"Be patient. You will understand someday," the Executive advised.

A woman stepped out the door and gave the Executive a hug. "Hi, Ruth. How are all my children?" he asked.

"They're all doing fine. They've missed you. If it were up to them, you'd be here every day. Oh, yes, all the older ones are doing well in school, and Jamie scored the winning free-throw last week."

"I wish I could have been there," the Executive said sadly. "But I was with some of the other kids. Is Don around?"

"No," Ruth responded. "He had to take Aaron to the doctor."

"Nothing serious, I hope."

"Just his booster shot."

"Good."

The Broker followed the Executive into the house. There, in the entry hallway, was a display of pictures— twelve children who appeared to range in age from four to seventeen. As the Executive walked through the house, he was clearly disappointed that more children weren't home.

"Wish I could be here when the others get home from school," he said to the woman.

"I know they'd love to see you, too," she responded.

"Grandpa, can we play trucks?" one of the boys asked excitedly as he tugged on the Executive's arm.

"Sure we can, Sport. Are they in the playroom?"

"Yes," the boy responded.

"Can I play, too?" the other boy asked.

"Of course." Then the Executive turned to the little girl, who had a "left out" expression on her face. "How about you, Sugar? You want to play trucks or should I read you a story a little later?"

The girl beamed. "I'd like a story, Grandpa."

The Broker watched in amazement as the Executive got down on the floor with the boys and played trucks, all the while accompanying his play with lifelike engine sound effects.

"That's quite the talent you have there," the Broker commented, just before a painful thought filled his mind. *I wish my dad had taken the time—just once—to play trucks with me.*

When the boys seemed to have had their fill of trucks, the Executive took the little girl in his lap and read a Dr. Seuss classic as the boys gathered around.

He finished the story, read another, then gave the three children one last round of hugs and headed for the door.

"Love you, Grandpa!" they shouted.

"I love you, too, with all my heart."

That must be what he means by 'touch,' the Broker thought. *I've never seen so much hugging.*

The Executive and the Broker got into the car and drove off. When they were no more than a block from the house, the Broker interrupted the silence. "Who are those kids, really? I mean, they're obviously of differing races, so they can't all be your blood relatives."

"You're right, but in my heart, they're all family. A few years back, it occurred to me that there are so many children with nothing. And I had been given so much. I decided that I had a wonderful opportunity to share. So I bought a house, renovated it, and turned it into a foster home for children who really needed some extra love and attention."

"Why do they call you 'Grandpa'?"

The Executive laughed. "I call them my 'grandchildren by choice.' They know that, so that's why they call me Grandpa. I love that title, so I try to give them as much time as I can. In fact, if I recall, I was on the phone with one of them the first time you phoned me. They're very important to me."

"I can see that! And the Georgia quarters you gave them? There's a message in that quarter for me, isn't there?" the Broker asked rhetorically.

"You're a good student," the Executive confirmed. "Those words all have special meaning to me."

The Broker guessed that he might be in for a "sermonette." He was. But he somehow didn't mind.

"Wisdom isn't something I've achieved on my own. I believe it's something I received from God. I could never have created and built this business on my own. I don't have a college education. I didn't even graduate from high school. But He gave me the wisdom, and because He did, my only choice was to return my business to Him. I simply see myself as a steward. I'm a caretaker—a manager of the things He actually owns. And it's my responsibility to manage it all to the best of my ability. Part of what He expects of me, I believe, is that I use these resources to help others."

"That's why you operate a foster home?"

"Right. As for Justice, I believe that my response to all His gifts—whether it's time, talents, wisdom, or money—is to give people a chance. It doesn't matter whether it's team members who need a college education, or kids who need love, or people of any race or color who simply need a fair shake; they'll only get what they need through real justice. Every day I get the opportunity to do something about it personally."

"What does Moderation have to do with all this?" the Broker asked.

"To understand Moderation, you have to understand extremism. Extremists care about only one thing. Making money is one example. Giving everything away is another. Neither pursuit yields any meaningful results. Extremists who only want to make money benefit only themselves. Extremists who choose only to give it all away can't generate anything new to give in the future. Extremists caught up in either trap have no time for spouses, families, friends, or relaxation. Moderation means that you balance it all in order to benefit all."

The Broker was pensive for a moment. "And here I thought the Georgia quarter was worth a mere twenty-five cents."

"If you remember one thing from all this, remember that every day is an opportunity. I had an opportunity to share some thoughts with my kids today that I hope will stick with them all their lives."

The Broker took out his palmtop organizer and made a few quick notes. He knew the Executive was offering him the keys to the generosity factor — he just didn't know how it all fit together. Perhaps through his notes he'd be able to figure it all out.

IO

THE NEXT STEP

U<small>PON THEIR RETURN TO THE OFFICE, THE</small> E<small>XECUTIVE WAS GREETED</small> by his Assistant and was handed a stack of phone messages.

"Do you mind if I return a few phone calls?" the Executive asked the Broker.

"No, not at all. Business is business."

"May I take you downstairs for lunch?" the Executive's Assistant asked.

"That would be great."

"We have a cafeteria on the main floor. Lunch is free for all staff members and guests. We have some terrific salads. You like salads?"

"You kidding? I'm from New York. It's usually either salad, fish, or great ethnic food for me!"

They went through the line, put their orders on cafeteria trays, and headed toward a table by a window that overlooked an outdoor patio, beyond which were trees that still displayed the last colorful hints of autumn.

"How's your day been so far?" the Assistant asked.

"Interesting. I'm pretty impressed that the Executive has provided a home for those kids who call him Grandpa. Must be pretty expensive to operate that place."

"Which one did you visit?"

"Which one? You mean there are more than the one I saw?"

"A dozen or so, actually. Of course, that includes the one in Mexico. And each facility provides a home for twelve kids, plus the couple who serve as Mom and Dad."

The Broker was again stunned by the math. "He's supporting more than 140 people in his foster homes?"

"More than 160, if you include the foster parents. He pays them to be full-time parents."

"Amazing."

The Executive had slipped into the cafeteria unnoticed and decided to join the conversation.

"Not so amazing," the Executive said. "It's simply a matter of seeing a need, being blessed with the resources required to meet that need, and then actually acting to meet it. It's one thing to think about ways to help others; it's quite another to act."

"The Executive is always teaching us that action is required," the Assistant added.

"You see," the Executive continued, "There's a big difference between held values and operational values. Held values are what people *say*. Operational values are what people *do*. How many times have you been disappointed by someone who talked a good game—'family values,' for example—but whose personal life reflected an entirely different set of operational values?"

"I can think of more than a few prominent politicians who fit that description," the Broker observed.

"It's not just politicians, though. It's pretty much all of us. We say we're not bigoted. But in the privacy of a conversation with close friends, we let a racist joke escape our lips. We say we care about our children. But we don't get involved in our schools. We say we care about the future of America. But we cheat on our taxes and are often too busy to vote."

"I think I know what you're talking about," the Broker admitted, trying to mask the fact that some of these "we-says" were hitting mighty close to home.

"It's very simple, really. One of my goals in life is to do everything possible to back my words with actions."

"In other words, you're saying that generosity is a key way to make certain that our held values and our operational values match?" the Broker wondered.

"You got it, Sport!"

The Executive and the Broker spent some time discussing the importance of action. The Broker took occasional notes on his palmtop.

Suddenly the Executive interrupted the conversation. "Speaking of action, we have to take some. We should be leaving for our trip to Leadville right now."

"Leadville? Never heard of it."

"It's beautiful. High in the mountains. You'll love it!"

"What's up there?"

"You'll see," was all the Executive said.

As they headed west on I–70, the Executive asked, "Are you interested in taking the scenic route? It'll take a bit longer, because we'll go all the way to Aspen instead of turning off at Route 91."

"I love Aspen," the Broker offered. "I've been skiing there several times over the years."

"It's a little early in the season for skiing, of course," the Executive observed, "but it's beautiful there any time of year. And the scenic route to Leadville is a real treat."

The Broker had no idea what he was getting himself into when he said, "Let's go for it, then." The "scenic route" was indeed scenic, but the Broker wasn't prepared for the hairpin turns and steep cliffs that seemed to drop off into nowhere.

I think I'm going to be sick, he thought as he checked his seatbelt and grabbed the edges of his seat.

"You okay?" the Executive asked.

"I'm fine." It was perhaps the biggest fib in the Broker's life, and he was relieved when they arrived in Leadville. "Quaint town," he observed.

"Lots of history here," the Executive noted. "When I was stationed at Fort Carson, we used to do some military exercises at Camp Hale. I fell in love with the Leadville area and promised myself that I would have a place up here someday."

"So we're here to see your mountain escape?" the Broker asked.

"Not exactly," the Executive replied as he drove through town and headed south. Several miles down the road, he turned onto a small side road and through stone gates and under a wrought iron sign bearing just two words: "Higher Hopes."

"This is it," the Executive announced.

"What is it? A wilderness church?"

The Executive laughed. "Far from it. You see, I've set up a foundation to provide a variety of services for kids. Up here, we have Higher Hopes Camp for boys and girls, we provide boarding for students who are going to school on our scholarship program, and we have another foster home."

"It looks like you'll come up with practically anything to be generous," the Broker chided.

"It's more than that! Higher Hopes gives kids a chance to develop and test new abilities. I want to do everything I can to make sure our future is filled with young men and women who have high self-esteem and the confidence to try new things."

"You can't meet the needs of every kid on the planet," the Broker reminded his host.

"True, but I can impact some. The Boys and Girls Clubs can meet the needs of some. Outward Bound can help some. Churches and synagogues can reach out to others. We're all in this together. I think we all believe that it's easier to shape our young people for success than to rehabilitate adults after they've failed."

"Makes sense to me," the Broker agreed.

The Executive gave the Broker an extensive tour of Higher Hopes. Near the end of the tour, he said, "I want you to meet some special people."

They drove to a dormitory building, parked, and walked into a comfortable reception area that served as a kind of gathering place for students. Several of the kids noticed the Executive and his guest and approached them excitedly.

"Are you speaking to us today?"

"Yes, as a matter of fact, I am."

"Great! We'll make sure everyone knows that."

A couple of minutes later, they were on their way to a small auditorium. A few students trickled in. Then a few more. By the time the Executive stood behind the podium to address them, about eighty students of high school age had taken seats.

"I want to talk to you about the most important transition any human being can make," the Executive began. "It's the transition from childhood to adulthood. Some people make the transition when they are 13, or 15, or 17. Some don't make it until they are 49, or 57, or 72. Some never make the leap at all."

The students were captivated by the words of the wise Executive.

He continued. "Some achieve great success at 24, or 32, or 41. But they never realize true significance. There's always something missing in their lives. There's always a gap between who they are and who they could become. What I'm saying is that while many people can achieve success, it seems to me that only a few achieve significance. My hope for each and every one of you is that you become the people that God wants you to become—that you discover the path to significance."

The Executive flipped the power switch on an old overhead projector and began to write on a blank transparency.

Success	vs.	**Significance**
Wealth		Generosity
Achievement		Service
Status		Relationships

"The success-motivated person tends to measure his or her life in terms of money, power, status, achievement, and recognition. The significant person places emphasis on a more spiritual view of life—generosity, empowerment of others, service, building up others, and helping them develop solid relationships.

"Let's take a closer look at the words I've written here. On the left side, you see the traits of a successful person—or at least what our society has told us are the measurements of success. On the right side, you see the traits of the significant person.

"The successful person has learned how to make money, but the significant person has learned how to give it away—how to be generous, to share the blessings of money with those who are in need or those who help meet a variety of social and humanitarian needs.

"The successful person has achieved great things—sadly sometimes at the expense of others. He or she is proud of what has already been accomplished. The significant person understands that the greatest thing anyone can accomplish is to serve others and to help them achieve their goals.

"Finally, successful people have attained a measure of status. Others look up to them and maybe even see them as role models. We often discover later that those who have become our role models let us down. They turn out to be something less than we had hoped. In direct contrast, the significant person is one who values relationships. They become trusted friends and invaluable mentors, and they invest their time in others rather than in striving to build status.

"If you look at them more closely, these components of significance all have something to do with generosity. Giving of resources is one form of generosity, serving others is another, and fostering meaningful relationships is yet another. It all comes down to Time, Talent, Treasure, and Touch."

Spontaneous applause erupted throughout the auditorium. Several of the students clearly understood how this profound philosophy had already impacted their own lives. The Executive smiled and continued.

"I can tell that many of you already understand what I'm saying. You place giving above taking. You volunteer to mentor the younger kids at Higher Hopes. You serve as counselors at summer camp. You may not have much 'treasure' at this point in your lives, but you invest your time, talent, and touch in the new kids who need you."

When the Executive's speech came to a close, he was approached by several students who shared wonderful stories about the younger children they were mentoring. The Executive was pleased that these students were investing their time in the lives of others.

On the way to the car, the Broker said, "This is truly amazing. You're passing your ideals along to these young adults so that they can keep them alive for future generations."

"You're exactly right. We all leave a legacy behind. I want to be remembered as a man who empowered others to put the generosity factor in action."

As they drove back to Denver, the Executive gave his passenger the facts. He explained that when the facilities of an old Boy Scout camp became available, he had to act quickly to make sure that they would continue to be put to good use. "Even back then, developers had an eye on the future and wanted to buy the land as an investment. But I was the high bidder and closed on the property within less than a month. We started the boys' camp right away. We added the girls' camp a couple years later. Last I heard, we've had almost 20,000 campers go through the program. As for the school, we've graduated more than 900 kids so far. The students who came to hear me talk today are fairly typical of the kids we sponsor. They are truly learning about the generosity factor, and they're going to be tremendous leaders some day."

"I think you're right. They will be. It's wonderful."

"The really wonderful thing is that every kid who comes here has the opportunity to hear about the love that God has for them, no matter who they are or where they come from."

"I somehow guessed that God would be a part of this," the Broker observed wryly.

"He's a part of everything I do. I wouldn't have it any other way. In His Word, He tells me to take care of His sheep—in other words, to be concerned about others—especially those who can't do it on their own. I can either act on what He tells me, or I can ignore it. I choose to act."

"It looks to me as though all the things you do—the scholarships, the foster homes, the camps—would really cut into your bottom line."

"It depends on how you look at it. I see profits as merely the score of the game, not the name of the game. My game is selling auto parts and service. If I do a good job of that, my customers give me their money in return. If I take exceptional care of my team members, they give their best service and their warmest smiles to the customers. If our Managers have a true opportunity to be successful, they give it everything they've got. The fact is, many of our Managers have decided that because they are successful, they want to be tithers."

The Broker was unfamiliar with the term he had just heard. "What's a 'tither'?"

"I almost hate to tell you," the Executive admitted sheepishly.

"Why?"

"Because it's another of those principles I've learned from my old-fashioned Bible, as you call it."

"I somehow knew that was going to be your answer," the Broker joked. "But what does it mean?"

"Very simply, it means that when we are blessed, a good way to express our thankfulness is through the tithe—giving ten percent of our income back to God and to the work He'd like to see done to help others. It's the least that I believe we owe Him out of our gratitude."

"So it's like a rule?"

"No, I see it more as a wonderful opportunity. It's a good habit to get into, just as it's a good habit to save and invest. Your best customers are in the habit of setting aside part of their income to take advantage of the investments you offer. I do the same thing, of course, but I also set aside a part of my income as my tithe."

"Do you expect your Managers to tithe because you do?"

"Not at all," the Executive replied. "They do it voluntarily. They understand why it makes sense. In fact, several of them give more than ten percent of their income. Anything given above the tithe is a true expression of generosity. It's what we call an 'offering.' I believe, as many of our Managers do, that it's not all about getting. It's about giving. It's been demonstrated over and over again that when you return to God what is His in the first place, His blessings will be poured out on you."

"So you give in order to get?" the skeptical Broker asked.

"No," replied the patient Executive. "I get in order to give. I'd be just as happy and content if our company had only one location. But because we have over 800 locations, we generate greater revenues and bigger profits. That means we have more to give. That means more money falls to the *real* bottom line—people who need help."

What planet is this guy from? the Broker wondered as he opened the car door, said good-bye to the Executive, walked into the hotel lobby, and took the elevator to his room.

"I'll pick you up in the morning," were the Executive's parting words.

11

HOME AND HEART

THE EARLY MORNING WAKE-UP CALL JOLTED THE BROKER OUT of a most pleasant dream about highly successful IPOs and soaring stock values. He fumbled for the light on his night-stand and switched it on. He glanced at his watch and re-alized that if he wanted to do some crunches to work on his abs before his shower, he'd have to get a move on. The Executive had promised to show up at the hotel no later than 7:00 A.M.

He had just finished tying his shoelaces when the phone rang a second time. It was the Executive. "I'm down-stairs," he announced cheerfully.

"You must get up awfully early," the Broker mumbled.

"I do. I've hardly missed a sunrise yet. Must have something to do with being raised on a farm."

The Broker rode the elevator to the lobby and spot-ted the Executive on the far side. He appeared to be hold-ing two paper bags. Upon closer inspection, he discovered they were bags from a fast-food restaurant.

The Executive held up the bags. "I brought breakfast."

"Are we eating in the car?"

"You got it, Sport."

The Broker chomped on the egg-and-ham-something-or-other as they headed out on the highway.

The Executive continued, "I figured you'd be hungry, and there isn't a good restaurant between here and my ranch. I thought we'd spend a nice relaxing day there."

"I thought you were just driving me to the airport. I'm going home today," the Broker protested.

"You can't. You'd miss my Sunday school class tomorrow. You'll learn a lot from it. You really have to be there."

"Well ..." the Broker hesitated. Then he thought more about the offer. "Okay, I'll stay if it's that important to you."

"It is. I'm going to introduce you to the most significant person in my life—my wife. She's a real treat!"

As they drove to the far outskirts of Denver, the Executive asked questions that made the Broker uncomfortable.

"Do you know any poor people—people in need—or do you associate only with people who are wealthy?"

"I know poor people. Or at least I know of them. I've seen them around."

"Who is the poorest person you know?" the Executive asked pointedly.

"I don't know. I guess my Driver. You know. My chauffeur. He's pretty poor. No, wait. It has to be that old bag lady who loiters outside my office building."

"You know a bag lady?" the Executive wondered.

"I can't say I actually know her. I just see her every day. She's very poor—always begging for money."

"And you give her some?"

"Of course not! I can't support laziness. I had her arrested the other day. She has no right to be there."

"So you're blessed and she's not," the Executive suggested.

"Blessed? That sounds like another one of your God concepts."

"In my mind, it is. That's why I try to remember my blessings every day. I try to recall them all. It isn't easy—I've had so many. As I told you, I believe they all come from God."

"Yes, you've made that point clear. Frankly, I don't see what all this has to do with the secret of the generosity factor."

"That's because you need to put all the pieces in place before you can understand any of them individually."

"Let's get on with it then," pressed the impatient Broker.

"Very well. Have you ever taken an inventory of your blessings?"

"You're suggesting that you have?"

"Of course. And I add to it every day."

"May I see it?"

"I'll share it with you, but first I'd like you to take your own inventory. You can do it tonight when you get back to your hotel. Then we'll consider our lists together tomorrow."

The Executive turned onto a side road that led through expansive grounds to a modest older home. The Executive parked in the front drive and led his guest inside.

The Broker was dumbfounded. "You live here?" was all he could say.

"Not what you expected?"

"No," the Broker admitted. "I expected a big mansion with mountain views. I mean, this is very nice, very comfortable...."

"Thank you," said the Executive. "This home was a gift, you know."

"A gift? You inherited it from your parents? It's your old family homestead or something?"

"No, it was given to me by the one who owns it all."

"God again, right?"

"You're catching on, Sport!"

A woman approached them in the family room. "This is my wife, Carolyn," the Executive said. "And this, Carolyn, is my new friend from New York."

"Pleased to meet you," Carolyn offered, "I've heard wonderful things about you. My husband tells me that you want to learn about the generosity factor."

"Yes, I do. But it seems I'm a slow learner."

Carolyn laughed. "Maybe you should tell him about the three 'M's first. After all, they play an important key in living a significant life."

"The three 'M's?" the Broker interjected.

"Yes," the Executive replied. "Master, Mission, and Mate. The three 'M's."

"I'm afraid you'll have to explain," the Broker admitted. "That wasn't covered in any of my college courses."

The Executive chuckled. "I'm sure it wasn't. For me, the three 'M's are the basics. I discovered my Master when I decided that God could do a better job of turning my life into something worthwhile and meaningful than I could on my own. So I put Him in charge. I had to finally admit that I couldn't control my life very effectively. In fact, I did a downright lousy job of it. But with God as my Master, I know I'm being guided through life by the one who created me. Surely He has to know what's best for me."

"You know that the whole 'God thing' is a stretch for me," the Broker admitted. "But I still want to hear about Mission and Mate."

The Executive was happy to continue. "My Mission became clear when I first took a night job at a small gas station in Wisconsin. I decided I wanted to serve customers by meeting their needs. That mission has been an essential part of everything I've done in the automotive business since then."

"Okay," the Broker chipped in, "I think I understand Master and Mission."

"If you understand those, you'll understand Mate. I wanted to find the right partner with whom I could share my life. We met when I was stationed at Fort Carson. She was an Army nurse and had the kindest, gentlest heart I had ever witnessed in another person. We fell in love and we decided almost immediately to spend the rest of our lives together. We just knew it was right. My wife is my perfect partner and companion."

"That's beautiful," the Broker confessed. "I wish I had that kind of relationship."

"I believe that's one of those things best left to God. You're no less of a person if you never find a mate. God may have another design for your life. But God's plan for me included Carolyn. Because we're right for each other, we have never once considered divorce. We've been married for over forty-five years, and I believe that's because we let God make the match. I thank Him for that every day."

"I know you probably believe God had a hand in that," objected the Broker, "but couldn't it be something more basic like love at first sight?"

The Executive laughed. "Could be that, too. All I know is I love her. And I want to live every day being generous with my love."

"He is, too," Carolyn added. "Not just toward me, but with so many others who need love."

"You'll always be number one with me," the Executive said as he lovingly and tenderly squeezed his wife's hand.

12

THE INVENTORY

WHEN THE BROKER GOT TO HIS HOTEL ROOM, HE TOOK A FEW moments to jot some brief notes in his palmtop computer. Then he checked his appointment calendar, and there, on its crystal-clear screen, he read the word "Theater."

A panicked thought flashed across his mind. *Stephanie! I had a date tonight with Stephanie! I'm in big trouble.*

The Broker placed a quick call to his rather upset friend. It required three distinct "I'm sorrys" to calm her down. *I'll have to find some way to make it up to her when I get home.*

Still upset by this atypical mental lapse, he changed into his exercise clothes, grabbed his swimsuit, and headed for the health center. He worked out on the treadmill, the rowing machine, and the stair-stepper. He lifted free weights. He hit the sauna. Then he jumped into the pool and swam twenty laps.

Normally, his mind would wander off on thoughts of current happenings in the market. This day, though, he was far removed from the markets. His thoughts came back to his day with the Executive.

Maybe I should think back on the so-called blessings in my life. Maybe I should make an inventory. He repeatedly dismissed these thoughts as quickly as they occurred to him.

Back in his room, tired but still exhilarated, he settled in under the covers to watch *Headline News*. Again the thought of an inventory came to him. *Naw*, he decided. *It's time for* CNN Sports*!*

He watched the scores—his favorite teams split 50/50 tonight—and the notion of taking an inventory of his personal blessings popped into his restless mind yet again.

Okay! All right already! I'll do it! his mind yelled at no one in particular. He reached over to the nightstand for a small tablet and one of the ballpoint pens provided by the hotel. *I'm sure they actually want me to steal this so I'm reminded of their hotel every time I use it.*

At the top of the page he wrote the words, MY BLESS-INGS: AN INVENTORY.

Then he began to list everything that seemed as though it could be counted as a blessing.

1. My house on Long Island
2. My business
3. The invention of the Internet
4. The view from my office
5. My apartment
6. My cars
7. My sailboat
8. My sport fishing boat
9. My art collection
10. My country club
11. My city club
12. My home theater
13. My golf pro
14. Stephanie (I hope!)
15. ...

On and on he wrote. He managed to fill three of the little pages in less than ten minutes.

"Enough, already," he muttered aloud. "That should satisfy him."

And with that, the Big Apple's most materialistic broker turned out the light, rolled over, and went to sleep.

13

GRATITUDE

"I DID WHAT YOU SUGGESTED," THE BROKER ANNOUNCED TO the Executive on Sunday morning—with no small measure of pride. "I made a list of my blessings last night."

"We're off to an early start. Even though the office is closed, let's stop by there for a few minutes," the Executive suggested. "That way you can share your list with me, and I'll share mine with you."

"Sounds good to me."

The Executive parked directly in front of the building. As the Broker got out of the car, he came face-to-face with a large block of marble that bore an embossed bronze plaque.

"I never noticed this before," the Broker observed.

"It's been here all the time," the Executive said with a grin.

"What does it mean, exactly?"

"It's our corporate purpose—it's why we're in business, you might say."

The Broker read the words on the plaque.

CORPORATE PURPOSE

1. To glorify God by being faithful stewards of all that is entrusted to us.
2. To have a positive influence on all who come in contact with our company.

Even his corporate purpose is all about giving and nothing about taking, the Broker thought to himself. Then aloud he said, "I think most companies have as their corporate purpose things like 'to be the leader in the industry,' or 'to manufacture a product with zero tolerance for defects,' or 'to get more dollars to the bottom line to keep the stockholders happy.'"

"Well, in our case, our ultimate stockholder is God, and I think He'd suggest that more companies should have a purpose along the lines of ours," the Executive observed as they made their way into the building and up to his office.

The Executive settled into a comfortable chair across a small table from the Broker. "What do you have there?" he asked.

"This is it," the Broker replied as he handed over his list.

The Executive studied the short list. He put it down on the table and managed a one-word response. "Interesting."

"How about your list?" the Broker inquired. "May I read it now?"

"No, I'm sorry, you can't."

The Broker practically sputtered his response. "You told me if I let you read my list, you'd let me read yours."

"Well, the truth is, I told you I'd share my list, and I will. I haven't written my blessings down. They're all in my head. And my heart."

"Okay, you did say 'share,'" the Broker conceded. "Please do."

And so the Executive began.

"My list is so long, and I don't want to bore you, so I'll just touch on the highlights. First of all, I'm thankful for God's unconditional love for me. I don't deserve it, but I'm its recipient anyway."

"And what else?" the Broker asked, hoping to finally connect all of the keys to the generosity factor.

"There's much more. For example, my blessings include the unselfish, faithful love of my wife, the births of my three children—especially my son Josh, who has Down's Syndrome. What a blessing he's been!"

"Blessing?" The Broker couldn't believe what he'd just heard.

"Yes. Wonderful blessing! Josh has shown Carolyn and me that everyone has value. That everyone has special gifts. Josh is one of the most loving, giving people I know."

"But the rest of your life is so perfect ..." the Broker blurted out without thinking.

"Please, please listen carefully. Josh is perfect, too. Our lives are so much richer because of him. God has used him to teach us about trust and about dependence. We've learned through Josh that every life is significant. God is the potter. We are the clay. And the clay shouldn't say to the potter, 'Why did you make me this way?' We need to learn to become thankful simply because we exist—for no other reason than that."

"Amazing!" the Broker acknowledged. "I know people who blame God because everything isn't perfect. And here you are, thanking Him."

"I thank Him because He owns it all. That means that everything is on loan from Him. Even Josh."

"I want to hear more about your inventory." The Broker wanted to learn, despite his many doubts.

"There are countless blessings," the Executive continued. "I'm thankful that so many of the children I've been privileged to help have turned out so well. I'm thankful that all the illnesses my wife, my children, and I have had over the years haven't been serious. Health is a wonderful blessing, and I'm grateful for every day on this earth!"

As he listened to the Executive, tears unexpectedly welled up in the eyes of the young, self-confident Broker. He tried to hide them. He was not sure he succeeded.

Then the Executive said something the Broker never expected. "And today, I believe I'm blessed that you came into my life. I'm thankful that I can play a part in teaching you about the generosity factor."

The Broker sat in silence. "I think I got this all wrong," he finally admitted. "When I counted my blessings, they were all 'things.' I can see that now. When you remembered your blessings, they were all gifts. Nothing you had earned yourself. Just gifts ... including your son Josh."

The Executive smiled. "That's right. Blessings really are gifts. And I'm just the steward of anything that's been given to me. I'm a caretaker. Because much has been given to me, much is required of me. That's my responsibility, and I accept it with gratitude."

"Your comment about me—do you really think that I'm one of your blessings?"

"I do. If I can teach you the why, the when, the where, and the how of the generosity factor, I believe you will make a lasting impact on the world. What a blessing that would be!"

The Broker didn't dare let his gaze connect with the Executive's eyes. He wasn't sure he was ready to become someone else's "blessing." He decided to steer the conversation in a different direction.

"I couldn't help but notice how many times I heard the words 'thankful' and 'grateful' in your inventory of blessings."

"That's the last of the keys to understanding the generosity factor," the Executive noted. "Because God has given me everything I have, I owe Him thanks. His gifts are beyond my imagination. In a way, they're indescribable! The more I realize that, the more thankful I become. The natural by-product of gratitude is generosity."

"I still don't quite understand how you can be thankful for everything, though. I understand about Josh, but there must have been some really bad things that have occurred in your life."

"You're right. My father walked out on our family when I was a young boy. That devastated me. Then I lost my brother in Korea. My first thought was, 'I can't be thankful for this.' But that's when it occurred to me that he truly was on loan from God, as are my life, my wife, my children, my business, my cars, this building, and everything else I can name. I decided to be thankful for the years that I had him in my life, rather than become angry about the years that he couldn't be part of my life.

"A great writer and teacher, Gordon McDonald, once said something like this: 'There are Driven people and there are Called people. Driven people think they own everything; and Called people believe everything's on loan. Driven people think they own their relationships, their property, and their businesses. They spend most of their time and energy *protecting* what they think they own. Called people know that even their relationships are on loan, so they spend time *fostering* those relationships.'

"I'm not driven to make money. I'm called to help others —through my business endeavors, through my giving, and by the very fact that my service centers provide jobs. We teach our team members vital life skills—they learn how to listen to the customers, how to recover from setbacks, how to work with others, how to exceed expectations, and how to be empathetic. We impart positive work attitudes and habits. We try to provide our team with a University of Life."

"I've never heard a perspective like yours before," the Broker observed as he made quick notes on his palmtop.

"It's really simple. A thankful heart tends to be a generous heart. A selfish person always asks, 'Why did this happen to me?' That leads to a 'victim' mind-set, and victims are never generous. They don't want to give. They simply want to get even somehow."

"What you're saying makes some sense, but I'm leaving early tomorrow morning and I still don't know what you mean by the 'generosity factor.' I don't understand the secret you promised, and, frankly, I'm a little disappointed that it isn't somehow more clear."

"It's all right in front of you. I've given you everything I can give you. Be patient, and you will eventually see it very clearly."

The Broker turned that last admonition over in his mind as they walked out to the Executive's car.

The last place the Broker expected to find himself on a Sunday morning when he could have been back in New York enjoying coffee with Stephanie—or on any other Sunday morning, for that matter—was in church. But there he was, not only in church, but in a small classroom filled with eighth-grade boys—rowdy, active, jean-wearing, gum-chewing teenagers.

Even more surprising was the fact that the Executive was their teacher.

How can a man as old as the Executive communicate with this bunch of energetic boys? the Broker wondered.

He didn't have to wonder for long. True, the Executive and the boys didn't share their style of dress, their haircuts, their music, or even their jargon. But they did share their love for each other, their mutual respect, and a close "brotherhood" that the Broker never knew could span so many decades.

The Executive quietly and patiently taught them about life using the Bible as the foundation of his lessons. They listened attentively, asked questions, and openly shared the challenges they faced at home and in school.

Amazing, the Broker thought. *He's passing his entire belief system on to these boys. And I'm sure the generosity factor is a part of what he teaches them. Someday, they'll pass this on to the next generation.*

The Executive ended the lesson with advice to the boys to work hard, treat people fairly, and do their best in all things. Several of them gave him spontaneous hugs.

After the last boy had left, the Broker asked, "Have you been teaching classes for very long?"

"I've been at it for more than thirty years. And many of my boys have become quite successful in life—loving husbands, good fathers, involved citizens. Some have struggled in life a bit more, but I'm still very proud of each and every one of them."

I'll bet you are, thought the Broker with a tinge of envy.

The Executive's wife joined the Executive and the Broker for the church service that followed Sunday school.

The Broker was once again struck by the obvious fact that Carolyn was as warm and endearing as the Executive was.

"We'd love to have you over to our house for lunch after church," she offered with a smile.

The Broker accepted without hesitation. "I'd like that."

The afternoon at the Executive's home was filled with comfortable conversation. The Executive showed the Broker around the grounds. He was especially proud of his horses, as well as his motorcycles and dirt bikes, but not for the reason the Broker had anticipated.

"My foster kids love the horses and the bikes. And I love to share them. I want the kids to experience a generous helping of adventure and challenge."

"I'm realizing that everything the article said about you is true," the Broker observed. "Giving really is the greatest joy in your life."

The Executive didn't see it quite that way. "Giving is not the greatest joy, of course, but it's right up there with my faith, my family, and my friends."

Despite his eagerness to get back to the fast-moving world of online trading, the Broker was nonetheless saddened to realize that his time with the Executive was drawing to an end.

And sure enough, his limousine arrived at the Executive's home at precisely the scheduled time.

"Thank you both for your warm hospitality," the Broker told the Executive and his wife.

"Our pleasure," Carolyn said with a smile.

The Broker shook the Executive's hand. "And thank you for sharing so much of your life with me. I have a lot of thinking and reflecting to do. I really do want to understand the generosity factor."

"You will," the Executive assured him. "I know you will. It will become clear to you." With that, the older man gave his student a big bear hug, catching him completely off guard. *He's like the dad I never had*, the Broker thought warmly.

As the young chauffeur pulled away from the Executive's home, the Broker turned to catch a last glimpse of his newfound mentor through the rear window.

What a remarkable couple, the Broker thought. *They're really changing the world for the better, one person at a time.*

"Will you be needing me tomorrow?" the chauffeur inquired.

"Yes, but only for the trip to the airport in the morning."

"Yes, sir. What time?"

"Oh, 5:30 or 6:00. My flight's at 7:30."

"Traffic can be heavy on Monday mornings, so I'll be here at 5:30, sir. But if you feel comfortable taking some extra time, that's quite all right. There won't be any additional charge. I'm just grateful I had the opportunity to meet you."

There was silence in the car as they drove. The Broker finally spoke. "You believe in God, right?"

"Yes, sir. Can't help it, given what He's done for me."

"And what's that?"

"Gave me another chance. Took away my drug habit. Found me a wonderful wife. Blessed me with two great kids. I didn't do nothing to deserve it, except turn my messed-up life over to Him."

"Really?"

"Yes, sir. Changed my heart. Changed my life."

"I wish it could be that simple in my life."

"It can be, sir."

Two left turns later, the hotel came into view. The Broker thanked the young chauffeur, gave him a handshake and a generous tip, and said, "See you in the morning."

Then he walked through the automatic doors and placed a quick call to his assistant on his cell phone. He connected with her answering machine.

"I'm arriving at La Guardia at 12:45 tomorrow afternoon, and I'd like to make sure my car is available. Thanks."

The Broker went to his room, watched ESPN for about an hour, then turned out the lights. He slept soundly through the entire night. He had no idea of the news that awaited him back in New York.

14

THE RETURN

THE BROKER'S FLIGHT LANDED ABOUT 1:10 P.M. IT WAS TWENTY-five minutes late, because of a minor air traffic control delay. The Broker could live with that length of delay—anything more than forty-five minutes tended to irritate him to the point where it ruined the remainder of his day.

This day, though, he was a bit less edgy, thanks to the oddly calming effect the Executive had exerted on him. There was, after all, some logic and reason behind the ideas the Executive had set out before him, even though he didn't fully understand the meaning of the keys to the generosity factor. There was some thread that tied them all together, he was sure, but he just didn't know what it was.

The Broker scanned the gate area for his Driver, then remembered that the Driver's Daughter might still be filling in and probably hadn't been told about the usual routine. He retrieved the one bag he had checked and headed for the street. No driver, no car.

He waited a few minutes, then dug out his cell phone and dialed the Driver's home phone number. A woman answered.

"I'm sorry, he's not here. He's already left for the church."

Who goes to church on a Monday afternoon? the Broker wondered. "How about his daughter?"

"She left with him. Most of the family members are already there. I'm bringing the two youngest boys over in a few minutes. Who are you, by the way?"

"I'm the Broker. I just arrived at La Guardia. I was expecting the Driver or his Daughter to pick me up."

"Then you don't know?"

The Broker was getting increasingly impatient. "Know what?"

"The Driver's wife died Friday night. The funeral is this afternoon at two."

The Broker was shocked. He carefully collected his thoughts. Then he spoke. "I'm sorry. I didn't know. I've been out of town for a few days."

"I understand. Sorry to be the one to tell you."

"That's okay. I needed to know. Can I ask where the service is being held?"

The woman told him, he took out his ever-handy palmtop, made a note of the information, and the conversation ended.

"Taxi!" the Broker yelled at the top of his lungs.

"This is the place. Pull over in front of that car," the Broker directed the cab driver as he spotted the gleaming black hearse in front of a small church in a low-income neighborhood.

The service was already underway when the Broker slipped in and sat down in the only remaining seat in the last row of the sanctuary. A rather large woman, backed by a choir, was singing an old spiritual. The Broker had never heard anything sung with so much emotion. He found himself fighting back the urge to cry.

A tall, slender man of advancing years stood up to speak. *Must be the minister,* the Broker thought. Indeed it was. He talked about the Driver's wife—about her tender heart, about how she could always be counted on to help others in need, even amidst the most trying struggles in her own life. He said that the Driver's family may not have been blessed with material wealth, but they had other riches that they shared freely and cheerfully. They gave of their time. They shared their talents.

"In fact," the pastor said, "if she could be with us today, she would have lovingly prepared and served the food we'll be sharing following the graveside service. That's the kind of giving woman she was."

The Broker thought back to his days in Denver and the words of the Executive—words that nearly mirrored what the minister was saying:

"The only way to give is to give cheerfully."

"Sometimes it's more meaningful to give out of your scarcity—to share those things that are in the shortest supply."

"No matter what your circumstances in life, there are things that you can give. Everyone can have an impact."

The Broker was drawn back into the moment when the minister asked the Driver to say a few words. He expected words of bitterness from the Driver—his wife's life had been cut short, after all—but what he heard stunned him.

"My wife was a gift from God," the Driver began. "Every new day with her was more special than the day before. I tried to tell her in all the ways I could how much I loved her. I'm glad I did, because I won't have any regrets about the things I might have left unsaid."

I had no idea my Driver was so eloquent, the Broker thought. *These are wonderful thoughts, especially meaningful at this sad time. They remind me of things the Executive said about every day being an opportunity.*

The Driver continued, with increased emotion in every word. "I've had so many blessings in my life. I thank God for all of them, great and small. I thank Him for my children, for my jobs, for my friends, for this church. But most of all, I thank Him that He gave me so many wonderful years with a woman who loved us all, and who took every opportunity to demonstrate her love through her actions. She was a rare and beautiful treasure. Like I said, she was a gift from God, and He now has the pleasure of her company."

As the Driver returned to his place in the front pew, the Broker couldn't help but notice the tears in his eyes—and the hugs he gave his children.

He's not the man I thought he was, the Broker observed to himself. *But he has his toughest days ahead of him. How is he going to manage with all those kids? Not one of them will ever make it to college.*

15

A NEW REVELATION

THE BROKER GOT OFF THE ELEVATOR TUESDAY MORNING AND walked briskly toward his office. As he passed through his private reception area, he noticed an attractive, well-dressed woman who appeared to be in her late fifties or early sixties. When he got behind closed doors, he summoned his assistant. "Who's the woman in the waiting area?"

"She claims to be a neighbor of yours."

"Oh, really? Long Island or my apartment?"

"I don't really know."

"I'm sure I don't know her. Please ask her to leave."

"I can't."

"Why not?"

"She says she won't leave until you see her. She's stopped by almost every day that you were in Denver."

"Really? Tell her I'll give her two minutes and then she's out of here."

"Will do."

The Broker settled into the high-back leather chair behind his desk and drummed his fingers impatiently while he waited for his assistant to usher the woman in.

She entered the Broker's office with a certain air of authority and seated herself in the chair closest to his desk.

He studied her for more than a brief moment. Finally, he asked, "Do I know you?"

"I'm your neighbor."

"I'm sorry. I just can't seem to place you, although I'll admit your face looks somewhat familiar."

"I live in your apartment building. Top floor. Three floors above you. I imagine you recognize me from the elevator."

The Broker was suddenly impressed. "You live in the penthouse? You have the whole floor?"

"I do."

This woman has it made, he thought. *She must have inherited a huge fortune to live in the penthouse. Or maybe she owns a hot new software company.*

"What brings you here?" he asked her.

The woman confronted him point blank. "Why did you have me arrested?"

The Broker was incredulous. "What?"

"Last Monday. The police hauled me in. They told me you called them and then actually faxed a signed complaint from your car. They told me you claimed I am a public enemy or something."

If the Broker's heart hadn't been so strengthened by his exercise regimen, he might have keeled over from a massive coronary on the spot. He stammered and stuttered for the longest time. All the while, his face was redder than the stripes on Old Glory.

"Y...y...you...you're the bag lady?"

"I am, if that's what you prefer to call me."

"But why?" he finally blurted out. "Why would you dress in old ragged clothes and leave that beautiful penthouse of yours to come down to the streets and hang out with the lowlifes? These people are dirty and poor—they're not like you at all."

"Oh, but they are," the Bag Lady replied softly. "I'm dirty and unkempt and poor."

The Broker protested. "But you live in the penthouse. You're dressed in fine clothes. How can you say that?"

"When I came into this world, I was naked and vulnerable and dependent. I was hungry. I was crying. I was covered with blood and my hair was a mess. Without someone else's help—the doctors, the nurses, and my parents—I would have been dead within hours."

"You're far from poor today, though," the Broker interjected.

"The truth is, I am not poor today. But money has nothing to do with it. Money isn't what makes a person rich. The people I meet in the street make me rich."

"You've lost me there."

"It's very simple, really. They've taught me about daily dependence on God. That makes me rich. They've provided a way for me to make a genuine impact—through my touches, through my words, through the small things I give them. I'm all the richer for that."

"Very moving, I guess. But why you? Aren't there homeless shelters that can help them?"

The Bag Lady hesitated. She wasn't sure at first that she wanted to give the Broker the full story.

"Aren't there?" he persisted.

"I know of several," she finally told him. "One is especially important to me. My parents started it many years ago, through a charitable foundation they established. For most of my life, I turned my back on what they held so dear. I enjoyed my inheritance—a grand social life, trips around the world with my many wealthy husbands, fine jewelry, and, of course, my penthouse. One day a big question crossed my mind. Why?"

"Why what?"

"Why was I privileged? What had I done to deserve my affluence? I hadn't earned it; it was a gift from my parents. Then it occurred to me that we all inherit what we have. It is all a gift from our Creator. It's all His in the first place."

I've heard these exact words before, the Broker thought. "Your solution, then, is to give it back to street people?" he asked.

"No. I don't give them money at all. A few quarters here and there, maybe. My financial support goes to a number of soup kitchens, homeless shelters, and other humanitarian causes."

"Why do you stand on the street, then? I see you day after day. You're telling me you don't give handouts?"

"If I stood in front of your building and handed out cash to the homeless, I'd solve their problems for less than a day. Would that money turn their lives around? Would they seek out the help they really need, whether it's help to break a drug habit or to develop some self-esteem or to get the education required to obtain a good job? No, what I do is meet people where they are—and I listen to them. Sometimes I cry with them and put bandages on their wounds. Then I point them in the direction they need to go. A shelter, a rehab program, a place where they can contribute of themselves and be housed and fed in return. Sometimes I'll give them an address and a subway token. In other cases, I'll escort them personally to make sure they get where they need to go. I always know that someone with a big heart is waiting on the other end to help them."

The Broker had caught only part of what she was saying. "That's it, then. That's your expression of generosity. But there are so many other ways you could have an impact. I still don't understand why you leave your beautiful penthouse every day and mingle with dirty, unwashed people."

"Very simply, my friend, I follow the example of Jesus, who lived several years of his life in the streets, roaming from town to town, helping every 'down-and-outer' He met."

"Why not leave that to the social workers and such? I'm sure you know some high rollers. Why don't you hold a charity event and invite some folks with big bucks?"

"Do you ever read the Bible?" the Bag Lady asked pointedly.

"I confess I haven't in the past, but I recently met a man who has nearly convinced me that I should."

"There are several Bible stories about generosity, but there's one that really touches me," the Bag Lady explained. "Jesus was in the Temple one day, and He watched the rich people parade in and give great amounts of money. Then a poor widow walked in and gave two small coins—the only money she had to live on. Jesus told the crowd that she had given more than all the others, because they had given out of their wealth, but she had given out of her poverty. I think what Jesus was saying is that real generosity isn't something that's carefully calculated. It's not something done for show. If it's genuine, it comes from the heart."

"I've been hearing that a lot lately," the Broker interjected.

"You see, my friend, I'm not looking for praise for anything I do. Jesus said that when we give to the needy, we're not supposed to announce it with trumpets. We're supposed to give as if our left hand doesn't even know that our right hand is doing the giving. It's called 'giving in secret.' That's how we learn to be generous without any underlying selfish motives."

The Broker was getting yet another picture of what generosity is all about. The bottom line is that it's about freely giving of everything you have. It's a willingness to give up position, rights, inheritance, authority, maybe even a part of the future—all to help someone in need.

"I could easily give money," the Bag Lady said, "but what these people really need are my heart, my time, my listening ears. Someone right out there in the streets with them to help heal them."

The Broker reflected on his conversations with the Executive—their discussions about Time, Talent, Treasure, and Touch. He saw how the Bag Lady gave of all of those commodities liberally. *Perhaps she has moved from success to significance because of that,* he thought to himself.

The Broker walked his new friend to the elevator and apologized from the depths of his heart for having had her arrested. "You've touched me in ways you'll never imagine," he told her. "I'm beginning to see how self-centered I've been. I'm not proud of it at all. But I think I can change."

"You're already changing, whether you realize it or not. I can tell you're beginning to understand some things about the true nature of generosity. You just have to take the next step and act on those feelings."

The woman stepped into the elevator and the doors closed. *Action is required,* the Broker thought on the way back to his office. *Where have I heard that before?* he asked himself rhetorically.

"Could I borrow your yellow pages?" he asked his assistant on his way through the reception area. He took the thick book, went to his office and closed the door. He flipped through the pages, found the category he was looking for, and began placing calls.

16

PUTTING IT ALL
TOGETHER

IT WAS ONLY 4:30 IN THE AFTERNOON WHEN THE BROKER checked off the last item on his electronic "to-do" list. He decided to use his "found time" at the club. He was sure that a good workout—followed by a sauna, steam, and swim—would have its usual wonderful effect on him. He was right. When he finished his routine, he decided he wasn't hungry and went directly to his apartment.

The night skies over the city were incredibly clear. The Broker stood at the window that looked directly over Central Park. He could easily make out The Plaza to the southwest and the George Washington Bridge farther off to the northwest. *I wish I could share this wonderful view with someone.* This was an oddly generous thought for the Broker—but the kind of thought he had been having more frequently since he had met the Executive. *It's a small thing, really, but I'd like to share it.*

As he reflected on his day, the Broker began to sense that true heartfelt generosity was more of a widespread phenomenon than he had originally believed. He had seen it in the Executive, of course, and the way he touched the lives of his team members, his foster children, and the kids who would have the chance to share in the wonders of camping experiences because of his involvement. He had also witnessed the simple sacrifices that flowed from the Driver and his family. And he had watched with amazement as the "Bag Lady" left her beautiful penthouse day after day to come to the aid of the destitute people who made their homes in the perpetually cruel streets of the city.

But he still didn't understand the key to the generosity factor—the key foretold in the Reporter's column and promised by the Executive.

Before he went to bed, he called Stephanie. "The view from my apartment is so beautiful, Stephanie. It's as if I'm seeing everything with new eyes and I want to share it with you. Could you come over for dinner tomorrow night? I'll make my famous Caesar salad." Bowled over by his invitation, Stephanie didn't hesitate for a moment to say "Yes."

The Broker was barely able to sleep that night as he turned countless thoughts over in his mind.

The next day, he went about business as usual, still pondering the thoughts that tumbled around in his head. Stephanie joined him for dinner, and as they stood on his terrace and gazed at the city lights, he realized that the day came to an end without any new answers ... or any new revelations.

It was mid-morning Thursday when he finally decided he needed some help to sort it all out. He placed a phone call to the Reporter.

"Did you go to Denver to meet the Executive?" was her first question.

"I did. I had a conference to attend, and he agreed to spend some time with me. Basically, I just followed him around."

"And...?"

"I learned some things about what he does and why he does them. But he promised that I'd discover the keys to the generosity factor. If I have, I sure don't know what they are."

The Reporter laughed. "It took me a while to put it all together. In fact, it was only after I studied all my notes for the sixth time that it hit me."

The Broker was anxious. "What is it?"

The Reporter toyed with him a bit when she replied, "You can read about it in my column next week."

"Next week? I can't wait that long. How about I buy you lunch and you share what you know with me?"

"You're on."

"I'll send a car for you. It'll be there by 11:45."

I wonder where he'll take me, the Reporter thought as she glanced at her watch. *"21," maybe? Or Tavern on the Green?*

At 11:40, she took the elevator to street level and watched for the car the Broker had promised to send. Sure enough, it arrived precisely on time. Much to her surprise, the Broker himself was seated in the back of the car.

"I didn't know you would be here. I thought you'd meet me at the restaurant."

"Maybe I'm a bit over-anxious," he admitted.

As the car pulled away from the curb, he rolled down the divider and introduced his guest to the Driver. "He's been with me so long that I feel as though he's family."

The Driver was quick to respond. "The Broker has always treated me fairly, but over the past several days, he's been especially kind and generous."

The Reporter was a bit surprised. "Really?"

"My wife passed away last week," the Driver explained. "Her funeral was Monday. The Broker stepped in to help my family immediately. By Tuesday afternoon, he had phoned an employment agency to find someone to help us around the house, meet the kids when they come home from school, cook our meals, and try to make things as normal as possible."

"You did that?" The Reporter was impressed.

"Someone had to help. Might as well be me."

The Broker queried the Driver. "How do you think she'll work out?"

"Too early to tell how the kids will adjust to a new woman in the house, of course," the Driver replied. "But I can't begin to tell you how grateful I am for your help. I don't know how I could manage without her."

The Broker glanced toward the rear view mirror, detected tears welling up in the Driver's eyes, and tried to console him. "I know it'll take time. If there's anything else I can do to help...."

"Thank you, sir. I really appreciate it."

The Driver maneuvered through the typical crush of Manhattan traffic as they continued to talk. The divider was never rolled up. A few minutes later, the Driver pulled the big car up in front of a restaurant on Broadway.

"We're here," announced the Broker.

"Nathan's?" the Reporter asked jokingly. "I gave up gourmet spaghetti in the staff cafeteria to have lunch at Nathan's?"

The Broker laughed. "I'm so weary of five-star restaurants. Sometimes there's just nothing like a big thick gourmet hot dog."

They ordered two of the juiciest kosher franks on the planet and found a corner booth. It wasn't quiet—Nathan's booths never are—but at least it was out of the way.

"I forgot how great these are," the Reporter commented just before she took another bite.

The Broker got right to the point. "I learned a lot about giving from the Executive, but I still don't understand his so-called secret. What is the 'generosity factor' anyway?"

"I'd be interested to know exactly what the Executive told you. Did you make any notes?"

"Sure did," the Broker responded as he retrieved his palmtop computer from his pocket.

The Reporter opened her notebook to a page she had flagged. "Let's compare notes. Let's see if he told you the same things he told me."

"Near as I can tell, his generosity is based on five principles, but they don't seem to be connected in any way. The first thing he told me is that 'He owns it all.' He's not referring to himself either; he's referring to God as the owner of everything."

The Reporter looked up with a smile. "That's exactly what it says in my notes. What do you have next?"

"He told me that 'Every day is an opportunity.' He said that he looks for new ways to impact the lives of others through generosity every day of his life."

"You're right on track so far. What follows that?"

"He said 'Action is required.' He pointed out that it's one thing to think about doing something, but it's another thing to actually do it."

"Amazing!" commented the Reporter. "So far, our notes compare exactly."

"Then he told me, 'Remember your blessings.' I have to confess that, at first, I didn't get this at all. He told me to make a list, and all I could come up with were material things. When he told me what was on his list, it put mine to shame."

"He had me make a list, too," the Reporter recalled. "Mine was also fairly materialistic, but I also managed to remember my health, my family, my friends, and the opportunity I had to get a good education."

"You did a lot better at that assignment than I did," the Broker admitted.

"What else?" asked the Reporter, knowing full well what the answer would be.

"He said 'Thank Him'—meaning thank God. He said that's the only way to remind ourselves that we're not at the centers of our own universes—that we're not really all that self-sufficient."

"Anything more?"

"No, not really. That was about it."

"Congratulations are in order, then. You hold the keys in your hand."

"Huh? I still don't get it."

The Reporter handed the Broker the page from her notebook. The five key points were neatly listed.

- He Owns It All.
- Every Day Is an Opportunity.
- Action Is Required.
- Remember Your Blessings.
- Thank Him.

The Broker stared at the sheet of paper with a blank look on his face.

"Don't you see it?" the Reporter asked in amazement.

"See what?"

"Look at the first letter of each of the five things the Executive told you."

"Aha! They spell HEART!" The Broker was relieved that he would no longer have to struggle with the mystery. "But this strikes me as rather trivial. After all, we all have a heart, don't we?"

"True, but we don't all have the same heart. Think about all the songs you hear on the radio. There are hard hearts, soft hearts, broken hearts, damaged hearts, empty hearts, bleeding hearts, cold hearts, cruel hearts, giving hearts, forgiving hearts, loving hearts."

"I guess so. I just can't believe it's all that simple. You mean to tell me that the generosity factor all comes down to heart?"

"That's the way I understand it."

"I'm sorry, but I fail to see how this so-called secret is going to change my life in any way, shape, or form."

"I think it's already happening. You've clearly demonstrated that you have a heart. You're impacting the lives of your Driver and his family. Just Tuesday—one of the 'every days' of your life—you saw an opportunity. You acted on it. You've already lived part of the secret."

"I guess you're right. And I have to admit that the satisfaction I got from helping someone else is a blessing in its own right. But I'm not ready to accept the fact that God owns it all or that I somehow have to thank Him for it."

The Reporter's response was candid. "I'm struggling with that myself, but at the core of my being, I'm an investigative reporter, not just a lifestyle columnist. I'm open to learning more."

The Broker lifted his Diet Coke in a toast. "I can buy that. Here's to learning more!"

Within minutes of his return to his office, the Broker decided to place a call to the Executive. True to his previous experience, his call was put right through.

The Executive greeted him warmly. "I was hoping I'd hear from you again."

"I think I understand the secret you've been trying to reveal to me," the Broker began.

"Really?"

"Yes. The phrases you gave me begin with letters that spell out the word 'HEART.' Is that it?"

"That's it."

The Broker protested. "Despite the fact that it took me some time to figure that out, it all seems incredibly simple."

"On the surface it is," the Executive agreed. "The real key to generosity, though, is more than simply 'HEART.' "

"I knew it! I knew there was more to it."

The Executive wished he could have been face-to-face with the Broker at that moment. He began, slowly and deliberately.

"The ultimate secret is a *changed* heart."

"Changed? How does it change?"

"It's really all about *Who* changes it," the Executive explained. "To me, a changed heart simply means being in sync with God. The reason I understand that He owns it all—the reason I thank Him—is because He's changed my heart. It's in sync with Him."

"I'm afraid you'll have to explain."

The Executive thought for a moment. "I noticed that you carry a palmtop organizer with you all the time."

"That's right. In fact, I depend on it."

"How do you make sure that the information in your palmtop organizer is accurate, up-to-date, and complete?"

"I think I hear what you're really asking," the Broker responded. "I simply connect it to my desktop computer and synchronize the files—addresses, calendars, notes, all of it. Any new information on my computer gets transferred to my palmtop."

"And what if you've entered new information directly onto the palmtop?"

"Well, it's a two-way deal. The new handheld data goes onto my desktop computer."

"That's exactly the way our hearts synchronize with God. He 'downloads' His information—through His message in the Bible, through our inborn consciences, and through the influence of others. We upload our information to Him through prayer, through lives of service, and through generosity. It's a two-way deal, too."

"Interesting," the Broker conceded.

"The really interesting thing about it is that a changed heart is a generous heart. The old way is to desire to have the good things flow toward us. The new way is to want the good things to flow out of us. As a result, even greater things flow into our lives."

"I have to admit this is all foreign to me."

"Remember when I spoke to the kids at Higher Hopes?"

"Yes."

"Remember what I wrote on the overhead transparency?"

"Vaguely."

The Executive explained again how important it is to make the transition from success to significance. The Broker could visualize the overhead transparency in his mind.

Success	vs.	**Significance**
Wealth		Generosity
Achievement		Service
Status		Relationships

"When you are 'in-sync' with God's purpose and plan, the words in the right-hand column describe you. But if you measure yourself in terms of wealth, achievement, and status, you're into a never-ending game. The more you get, the more you want. Enough is never enough. But if you focus on spiritual significance, you realize that you're already loved and accepted—and love and acceptance are the greatest things anyone can possess."

The Broker listened intently. He asked questions. He probed with the mind of a skeptic. He told the Executive about his Driver, about the Bag Lady, and about the other selfless people he had encountered lately. He admitted that he sensed that there was some underlying truth that connected them. He wondered if that connection might be their changed hearts.

"How will I know when I have truly attained significance?" the Broker asked when their conversation was nearing the end.

"You will know by the sincerity of your generosity, by the joy you find in service, and by the selfless nature of your relationships. You will know by the depth of your changed heart."

It didn't take the Broker long to realize that his heart really was changing. In a manner of speaking, his "palm-top" was getting synchronized with God's "desktop." He decided that God's principles really could work in his own life. All he had to do was accept them as truth. He concluded that his profound success really was a gift from God, and that God indeed owns it all. He began to look at every day as another opportunity to care and to give. He acted in concrete terms at every opportunity. He discovered that his real blessings weren't the material things of life after all.

In the days, weeks, and months that followed, the Executive guided the Broker through the wonders of the generosity factor and taught him how to deepen his newfound relationship with God.

The Broker discovered exciting new ways to share his blessings both personally and corporately every day. And every day on his way to his office, he stopped for a moment and looked up past his towering office building as a few brief, simple words crossed his mind.

Thank you for the gift of the Executive. And thank you for gently and patiently leading me on a journey from mere success to real significance.

17

THE FUTURE STORY

A PERSONAL NOTE FROM KEN BLANCHARD

How many times have you read a book or watched a movie and asked yourself, "Is that really the way it ended?"

We all try to write our own endings to stories—especially the ones that leave some things unresolved.

"Did the boy get the girl?"

"Did the girl get the boy?"

"Did they find success, meaning, and significance in their lives?"

"Did they live happily ever after?"

I'm going to save you the trouble of having to answer those questions on your own. I'm going to give you the answers. Because I took part in creating these characters and the experiences they've had, I feel I have that right. You can agree with my ending, or you can write your own. But here's what happened to the people in *The Generosity Factor*.

The Reporter continued to write stories that touched the lives of others as well as her own. Her series of articles about the Executive ultimately were turned into a best-selling book that won her widespread critical acclaim—along with a Pulitzer Prize.

The Driver struggled at first. Despite the wonderful contribution of the live-in daycare provider that the Broker found for him, he had tremendous difficulty juggling his responsibilities at home with his need to make money and provide for his family. He needed to meet the emotional needs of his younger children, who simply didn't understand why their mother had "gone to heaven."

Though he lived a lonely life for almost three years, the Driver eventually remarried. His new wife is a loving, caring, giving lady, who is raising his children as her own. At first, the children were hesitant to accept her. Their feelings for their mother were too strong. But she won them over, with steadfast patience and unconditional love.

The Driver's Daughter went to college and completed her degree, thanks to a scholarship provided by the Broker. She went on to earn her MBA and eventually joined the Broker's firm as a technical analyst. From the very beginning of her career, she made immeasurable contributions to the Broker's ongoing success.

Stephanie and the Broker continued to see each other for several months and still remain "long-distance friends" today. She was so moved by the changes she saw in his life that she eventually quit her investment banking job and moved back to her hometown of Minneapolis, where she is now the executive director of a large, well-known charitable foundation.

The Bag Lady still hangs out in front of the Broker's office building. She and the Broker exchange knowing glances and warm smiles every day. He is careful not to expose her for who she is. She remains steadfastly devoted to stepping out of her comfort zone to help the disadvantaged with her tender touch, her compassionate words, and her wide-open heart. Her effectiveness has been enhanced by the Broker's involvement—he supports her favorite shelter financially and volunteers one night a month to serve a hot meal to the homeless.

The Broker is, in short, a new person. Early in his career, he worked to live. Then, as he got caught up in the pursuit of wealth and grandeur, he lived to work. Today, he lives and works to give. He is still unmarried and childless and has placed his assets into a trust that will provide ongoing resources for a wide variety of worthwhile causes.

The Executive continues to touch one life at a time—through scholarships, through foster homes, through adopting "grandkids," through creating new lives for kids through Higher Hopes Camp and School. He still teaches thirteen-year-old boys at his church about the love of God. He still tells them that if they want to be leaders in life, they must learn to become servants. He still shares the principles of "HEART" with anyone and everyone who will listen.

As you've read our ending, it's entirely possible that you may have seen things differently. You may have devised your own ending. You may imagine that something different happened to the Reporter, the Driver, the Driver's Daughter, Stephanie, the Bag Lady, or the Broker.

On top of all that, you may have concluded that a person like the Executive could not possibly exist in real life. "His story is as phony as they come, because it's simply too good to be true," you may say. If so, I have news for you!

The idea of writing a book on generosity had been in the back of my mind for quite some time. The reason I never began writing it is because I couldn't come up with a clear example of how generosity fits with modern-day notions of success. Is there such a thing as the generosity factor—some tangible relationship between giving and significance? I simply didn't know.

Then, out of seemingly nowhere, I met a man who appeared to express the principles of HEART in his daily living. At first I thought he, indeed, was too good to be true. So I quietly studied him—his life, his giving habits, his care and concern for others—and it all rang true.

This man, like the Executive in our story, operates twelve foster homes and has "adopted" hundreds of children. This man, like the Executive, has started a camp for kids—not in the mountains of Colorado but in the forests of northern Georgia. This man has handed out over sixteen million dollars in scholarships to his team members or employees of his stores. This man has taught Sunday school to boys not for thirty years, but for over forty. This man is the founder of a successful business with more than 1,000 facilities, as compared to the 800 fictitious service centers operated by the Executive in our story.

Above all, this man still tells the people he meets about the "Three 'M's"—Master, Mission, and Mate. And because he "walks the talk," he has created a foundation that will continue to touch young lives, one at a time, well into the future. He does this without any fanfare, without any desire for recognition. He agreed to participate in this book if, and only if, the setting and situations were changed so that the story didn't reflect a literal account of his life. He's not looking for praise. He simply wants us all to understand and apply what he has learned about the generosity factor.

This remarkable man—the embodiment of the Executive—is my coauthor, my dear friend, and the founder of Chick-fil-A, S. Truett Cathy.

Thank you, Truett, for the profound impact you have had on my life. Thank you for teaching us that the journey from success to significance takes place, to a great extent, when we put *The Generosity Factor* into practice.

ACKNOWLEDGMENTS

Ken would like to acknowledge the involvement and support of a number of people:

S. Truett Cathy, whose friendship has enriched my life and whose servant heart has inspired so many to do more than they ever imagined they could do.

My wife, **Marjorie Blanchard**, who is my love, my partner, my inspiration, my life.

My son, **Scott**, my daughter, **Debbie**, her husband, **Humberto**, and my grandchildren, **Kurtis** and **Kyle**, who bring me profound joy and make me proud.

Mark Miller, vice president of training and development for Chick-fil-A, who quickly captured the vision for the book. Without Mark's steady hand of guidance, this project never would have happened.

Steve Gottry, a friend and collaborative partner who loves to create characters and tell stories, for combining his enthusiasm and writing skills to bring the concepts to life.

Don Perry, vice president of public relations for Chick-fil-A, who walks the talk and who served as a catalyst to make the project a reality.

Dottie Hamilt, my more than capable "right hand," whose infectious attitude and can-do spirit enhance my life in so many ways.

Margret McBride, my friend and long-time literary agent, who shepherds my books through the involved publication process.

Thanks to you all!

Truett would like to add his word of thanks to the following people:

Dr. and Mrs. Charles Carter, who both have had a great influence on my life; Dr. Carter as my pastor for 27 years and Margaret as my executive assistant for more than 17 years.

J. B. Fuqua, who taught me that "the more you give, the more you have." He has lived this truth throughout his life.

Jeannette Cathy, my treasured wife. She taught me early in our marriage the importance of tithing.

My three children, **Dan, Bubba,** and **Trudy,** have demonstrated that it's impossible to "outgive" God.

There are several other behind-the-scenes individuals whose contributions merit recognition.

Thanks to **Lyn Cryderman, John Sloan**, and **Verlyn Verbrugge**, who together have cared for this book through Zondervan to its publication.

Production assistants/proofreaders: **Bonnie Hodgson, Linda Purdy, James Gottry, Heather Isfan, Becky Monrean,** and **Dave Gjerness.**

ABOUT THE AUTHORS

Ken Blanchard, Ph.D., is the Chief Spiritual Officer (CSO) of The Ken Blanchard Companies, Inc., a management training and corporate solutions company with headquarters in San Diego and offices around the world.

Ken is a world-renowned speaker and the author or coauthor of several best-selling books, including *The One Minute Manager®, Raving Fans, Gung Ho!, Leadership By the Book,* and *High Five!* His books have combined sales of more than twelve million copies and have been published in more than twenty-five languages. In 1996, four of Ken's books appeared on the prestigious *Business Week* bestseller list at the same time—a feat that has never been equaled by any other author.

In 1999, Ken, along with Phil Hodges, founded The Center for FaithWalk Leadership, an organization dedicated to the goal of empowering leaders of faith to apply the principles of "servanthood" in their business and personal lives.

Ken and his wife, Dr. Marjorie Blanchard, head of The Ken Blanchard Companies' "Office of the Future," have established a unique corporate giving program that enables each of their team members to research and designate specific charities to be the recipients of a significant portion of company profits.

To obtain additional information on The Ken Blanchard Companies, Inc., refer to their Web site, www.kenblanchard.com.

To learn about The Center for FaithWalk Leadership, log on to: www.faithwalkleadership.com.

Services offered. Ken Blanchard speaks to conventions and organizations all over the world. The Ken Blanchard Companies offers extensive training and team-building programs that build on the principles of his best-selling books. In addition, the companies conduct seminars and in-depth consulting in the areas of teamwork, customer service, leadership, performance management, and quality.

For further information and Ken Blanchard's activities and programs, please contact:

The Ken Blanchard Companies
125 State Place
Escondido, CA 92025
(800) 728–6000 or (760) 489–5005
(760) 489–8407 (fax)

S. Truett Cathy is the founder and chairman of Chick-fil-A, Inc., now a billion-dollar-plus quick-service restaurant chain with more than 1,000 locations, currently in 34 states and Washington, D.C.

Truett is well known for his heartfelt generosity—in terms of time, talent, touch, and treasure. His WinShape Centre® Foundation currently provides long-term foster care homes for more than a hundred children; Camp WinShape®, a summer camp program for boys and girls; and WinShape Wilderness®, an experiential learning organization. The foundation has also funded hundreds of college scholarships as part of a co-op venture with Berry College in Rome, Georgia.

A Sunday school teacher for nearly fifty years, Truett has invested thousands of hours with hundreds of junior high school-age boys. And he has shared his hugs ("touch") with scores of "adopted" Grandchildren by Choice.

His company is the sponsor of the Chick-fil-A Peach Bowl® and Chick-fil-A Charity Championship® hosted by Nancy Lopez. These events are among the most popular in the college bowl arena and on the LPGA Tour schedule.

Chick-fil-A, Inc., provided its franchisees the opportunity to enter an agreement to operate a Chick-fil-A restaurant with a minimal, refundable financial commitment of only $5,000. It's not surprising that the retention rate of restaurant franchises is historically around 95 percent. Also of interest is the fact that the retention rate of hourly restaurant employees is one of the highest in the "fast food" industry.

For more information on Chick-fil-A and Truett Cathy, you may go to the Web site: www.chick-fil-a.com. To order Truett Cathy's new book on the Chick-fil-A business story, *Eat Mor Chikin: Inspire More People*, please visit your local bookstore.

PRAISE FOR THE GENEROSITY FACTOR™

Truett Cathy is without a doubt a leader when it comes to generosity! And his partnership with Ken Blanchard brings an intriguing story about the power of giving. Through characters we can easily identify with and learn from, this book shares truth that when applied will take you to the next level—from success to significance.

—DR. JOHN C. MAXWELL
FOUNDER, THE INJOY GROUP

If Ken Blanchard writes it, it's good. If S. Truett Cathy writes it, it's good. When these two giants team up to produce *The Generosity Factor*, they introduce a practical, workable, God-centered approach to moving from success to significance. Good stuff. Easy to read, fun to follow, blessings abound!

—ZIG ZIGLAR
AUTHOR AND MOTIVATIONAL TEACHER

The value of generosity is important to cultivate, and I believe this book portrays it in a meaningful way. This is indeed the kind of reading people need today. Ken and Truett are skilled in saying just the right thing at the right time. This book will help a lot of people.

—RUTH STAFFORD PEALE

Truett Cathy is qualified to write about the Generosity Factor. He lives it! He is generous with his money, but more than that, he is generous with himself. Usually, Truett does not publicize his generosity; he is a quiet practitioner. As fellow worker, friend, and employee for thirty-two years, I have observed the impact of his generosity to thousands of people. But I have been more than an observer; I have been a recipient of Truett Cathy's generosity. If you want to learn about the Generosity Factor, Truett Cathy can teach you.

—JAMES L. S. COLLINS
FORMER PRESIDENT OF CHICK-FIL-A, INC. (RETIRED)

I am blessed to know the "Executive!" And to have once been the "Driver" and to understand the "Broker"! The characterization of these people is sure to capture the reading audience and involve them in the excitement and life-changing experience of the Broker! In two periods of about one hour each I read it all! I am thrilled to see this message being sent out in the powerful way that I believe will make it valuable to any serious reader who will take the short time required to read it. The quick, easy "readability" of *The Generosity Factor* is sure to make it take hold of the lives of countless people and change them for all eternity!

—DR. JAMES W. DYER
SENIOR MINISTER EMERITUS
SOUTHWEST CHRISTIAN CHURCH, EAST POINT, GEORGIA

The Generosity Factor tells the story of a Colorado businessman who seems almost too good to be true. In fact, the real-life model for this portrait is even more remarkable than the fictional version. The real story takes place in Georgia, not Colorado, and the fictional "Executive" closely resembles S. Truett Cathy, the founder of Chick-fil-A, Inc., a man who has long lived by the Christian faith and moral principles outlined in the narrative. The book tells a true story in the form of an engaging parable, and any reader can benefit from this authorial partnership between Ken Blanchard and Truett Cathy himself.

—SCOTT COLLEY
PRESIDENT, BERRY COLLEGE. ROME, GEORGIA

The Generosity Factor is a story about truths that can change our culture economically, socially, morally, and spiritually. These principles can, when employed, help the successful person who lacks a sense of significance find fulfillment. The subject is timely. The style is tantalizing. The substance is transforming. In summary, it is a terrific book deserving of the reader's time.

—DR. NELSON L. PRICE
PASTOR EMERITUS, ROSWELL STREET BAPTIST CHURCH, MARIETTA, GEORGIA, AND CHAIRMAN, INTERNATIONAL BOARD OF TRUSTEES, FELLOWSHIP OF CHRISTIAN ATHLETES

What a wonderful book! *The Generosity Factor* is most inspiring! It makes you want to examine your life and make it better. It indeed lets one know "it is more blessed to give than to receive." Winston Churchill said, "We make a living by what we get, but we make a life by what we give."

—DR. BILL SUTTLES
PRESIDENT EMERITUS, GEORGIA STATE UNIVERSITY

This is a delightful little book! So clear and simple, yet so incredibly profound. I recommend this book to all who seek a satisfying life and wonder why they don't have it despite their apparent "success."

—BOB CRUTCHFIELD
PRESIDENT/CEO, CHRISTIAN CITY, ATLANTA, GEORGIA

The Generosity Factor is a book sprinkled with poignant examples of how the Lord intervenes in our lives when we seek His will and give unselfishly. This book should appeal to many who don't know the value of sharing and giving back a portion of what He has given to us. A must for your reading list.

—EDDIE J. WHITE
ASSISTANT SUPERINTENDENT FOR PERSONNEL (RETIRED),
CLAYTON COUNTY (GEORGIA) PUBLIC SCHOOLS

I have just finished reading *The Generosity Factor* and was touched by the simple, yet profound, message. How wonderful it would be if this book inspires others to understand and to develop the generous spirit outlined in this book. Our nation has many children whose lives can be touched and changed one by one. Having known Truett Cathy personally for many years and having worked with him as he developed his foster care program, I can honestly say that he is the most humble and generous man that I have ever known. Mr. Cathy has made a difference in the lives of too many children to even count, and he will continue to enrich the lives of so many more. For the sake of our children, I pray that his efforts will be duplicated many times over.

—RUTH WILLIAMS
RETIRED DIRECTOR, COBB COUNTY (GEORGIA) DEPARTMENT OF FAMILY
AND CHILDREN'S SERVICES

This book is a powerful aid to anyone who should have a personal philanthropy program as part of his or her lifestyle.

—J. B. FUQUA
ENTREPRENEUR AND PHILANTHROPIST